The Light Infantry Regiments

During the Seven Years' War bodies of 'Light Troops', raised by Amherst and Wolfe, acted as skirmishers and scouts in the forest wilderness of North America. Recruits were selected from athletic and intelligent young men of regular Line battalions, especially excellent marksmen. These troops soon learnt the value of adapting clumsy contemporary uniform clothing to suit their specialised duties. Bulky long-skirted coats were hacked short, Indian-style leather leggings were adopted to protect legs from undergrowth, and the brims of cocked hats were slashed off to make caps more suited to woodland skirmishing. Efforts were made to provide them with lighter weapons such as the Royal Artillery carbine, and they used Birmingham-made tomahawks and knives. The emphasis was on mobility and self-sufficiency, avoiding stylised tactics depending on blind obedience to old-fashioned drill books.

There were also larger formations, such as the 80th Foot, raised as a so-called 'Light Armed Regiment'; the 85th 'Light Infantry Volunteers' and the 119th 'Prince's Own Light Regiment'. The latter, painted by the Swiss artist Morier, wore the short-skirted coat, tight breeches with half-gaiters, lighter equipment, and metal-mounted helmets which were to be characteristic of the evolution of light infantry costume. To what extent these battalions were 'light infantry' in the specialist sense we do not know; in any event, they were disbanded at the end of the Seven Years' War. However, in 1755, a more important step had been taken. In America a regiment was raised from German, Austrian, and Swiss settlers with hunting and wilderness experience. Initially

known as the 62nd, it was re-numbered the 60th Royal American Regiment in 1757, and from its conception had specialised 'light troops' connotations.

Initially trained by the Swiss officers Lt. Cols. Henri Bouquet and Frederick Hallimand, it rapidly expanded in strength to four battalions. The third and fourth battalions were raised partly in Hanover, and before long all were provided with specialist rifle companies dressed in green.

Around 1777–1779 independent companies of expert backwoodsmen were raised in America. Known as 'Rangers', their function was to provide irregular scouting parties operating behind enemy lines, attacking and destroying baggage

Jacket worn at Waterloo by Lt. H. Anderson, light company, 2/69th Regiment. Of scarlet cloth with willow green fa[cings] it has gold lace and buttons; note curiously shaped turr[...] ornament, in gold on green, and placing of buttons o[...] pleats. When first exhibited in 1890 it was accompani[ed by] a second jacket completely without lacing of any kind [...] to be Anderson's undress coat. The wing shown here [...] with gold lace and a silver buglehorn.

and a plethora of styles of jaunty leather caps embellished with badges, roaches, crests and metal reinforcement. They began to use buglers instead of drummers, carried tomahawks and knives, used powder horns, and were trained to operate in an independent rôle. As a consequence the 'light bobs' became fashionable, and wealthy young men vied to become officers in such units.

Writing in 1788, David Dundas pointed out that most, if not all, European armies then used Light Infantry, and that they tended to form theirs into separate corps rather than use them as élitist additions to Line battalions.

In 1794 a regiment of volunteers, mainly drawn from superior Fencible units[1], was raised as a private venture and was placed in the Line. This was the 90th (Perthshire Volunteers) Regiment which, from its formation, was considered a true regiment of Light Infantry, and was dressed accordingly, with helmets and short clothes. In 1798 this regiment was on Minorca; Sir John Moore, who had local command, watched it

[1]See Men-at-Arms 114, 'Wellington's Infantry (1)' for explanation of different classes of volunteer and militia units at this period.

trains and supply dumps. Many such units were raised before and during the American War of Independence. Dressed in green and blue and with Indian-style deerskin appointments, they gained an enviable reputation for skill, daring and ruthlessness.

Notwithstanding the high success rate of these 'light units', the Horse Guards generals, ever conservative and cautious, showed little enthusiasm for a continuation of unorthodoxy, although the addition of light infantry companies to the battalions of Line infantry had become permanent features of the establishment by 1770. During the War of Independence it became popular to mass several such companies together to form élite 'light' battalions. As they developed, the light companies adopted short jackets, fancy waistcoats

Jacket of a lieutenant-colonel of the 52nd Light Infantry, c. 1812–15; it has buff facings, buff turn-backs, silver buttons, and white shalloon lining. Another example of an officer's jacket of this regiment shows the same details, except that the insides of the lapels are scarlet rather than buff, so that when buttoned back as illustrated it would show a completely scarlet front. This second, undress jacket had a similar back to the service version illustrated: two buttons at the waist, with two pairs below set on a white piping on the pleats, and a third white piping along the vent edge. False three-point pocket flaps were edged with white piping on three sides.

MEN-AT-ARMS SERIES

EDITOR: MARTIN WINDROW

Wellington's Infantry (2)

Text and colour plates by

BRYAN FOSTEN

OSPREY PUBLISHING LONDON

Published in 1982 by
Osprey Publishing Ltd
Member company of the George Philip Group
12–14 Long Acre, London WC2E 9LP
© Copyright 1982 Osprey Publishing Ltd
Reprinted 1983, 1984, 1985, 1986 (twice), 1987

ISBN 0 85045 419 0

Filmset in Hong Kong
Printed in Hong Kong through Bookbuilders Ltd

Author's Note:
**This book is the second of two volumes. The
first, Men-at-Arms 114, dealt with the establish-
ments, organisation, daily life, drill, weapons
and equipment of the British infantry as a whole,
and the colour plates were devoted to the uniforms of the Foot Guards and 'English' Line
regiments. This book deals with the formation,
and brief service records of the Light Infantry,
Highland, West India, Garrison and Veterans
regiments, and with the King's German Legion
infantry. The colour plates are devoted to these
units. Volume 1 included a brief list of regimental facings and lace arrangement for the Line
as a whole, taken from De Bosset, 1803; this book
includes a much fuller table taken from Hamilton Smith, 1812. Photographs and drawings
relevant to the uniforms of all types of infantry
units will be found in both volumes.**

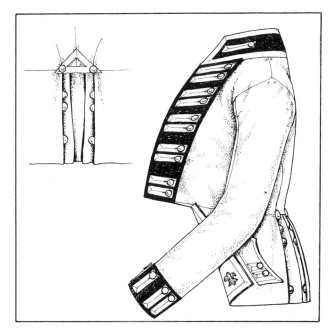

executing specialist field exercises and became so impressed that he noted and used some of the basic principles when he prepared his paper on the training of Light Infantry and Rifle Corps some five years later.

The Foot Guards were following suit: by 1794 they had light companies. The 1st Regiment had four at one time, and the 2nd and 3rd Regiments had two companies each.

The Duke of York, ever ready to innovate, began a study of the value of specialist light troops as early as 1797, and it was under his aegis that Sir Harry Calvert issued a memorandum recommending Horse Guards to form corps of light infantry. Even so, it was not until 1802 that Whitehall finally accepted the need which, as Dundas had reported 14 years earlier, meant that 'voltigeurs', 'chasseurs', 'tirailleurs', 'jägers', 'cacciatori' and 'caçadores' were already well established in other armies. Finally, they ordered that the 52nd Regiment, and subsequently the 43rd Regiment, should be transformed to Light Infantry.

In 1803 Sir John Moore was instructed to train these two regiments, along with the equally novel 'Experimental Corps of Riflemen'. Training was centred at Shorncliffe, Kent, where he commanded. The methods of training were partly devised by Moore, but appear to have been partly culled from earlier work in the field by the Swiss Maj. Gen. Baron de Rottenberg of the 60th Regiment. Moore's policy was to produce quick-thinking, intelligent, mobile soldiers capable of acting on their own initiative. Old-style drill manuals, which still governed the training of the mass of British infantry, were set aside; and discipline was maintained, at least to some extent, by appeals to pride in self and unit rather than by the lash.

43rd (Monmouthshire) (Light Infantry) Regiment

The regiment was converted to Light Infantry on 12 July 1803. A second battalion was raised in 1804. The 1st Battalion was at Copenhagen in

A copy of the jacket of Capt. Walter Clarke of the 95th Rifles, *c.* 1807–10, now in the Royal Green Jackets Museum at Winchester. Of dark rifle green with black velvet facings, it has black braid and silver buttons. Note particularly the wide sweep of braid over the shoulders and on to the back of the jacket; and the elaborate five-button cuffs.

Undress jacket of an officer of the 19th Regt., faced green, with silver buttons and white piping. The R.U.S.I. had a grenadier officer's jacket of the same unit and period which had rich, square-ended gold lace loops set in pairs—five pairs to each lapel—and white pipings on the lapels and slanting pocket flaps. The white turn-backs were edged with broad gold lace on green backing, and had gold grenade ornaments on green backing; there was a triangle of gold lace at the rear waist.

1807, and both battalions were with Moore, the 1st at Corunna and the 2nd retreating to Vigo. The 1st later served as part of the Peninsular Light Division; the 2nd Battalion was at Walcheren. In 1814 the 1st Battalion was sent to America, forming part of Pakenham's force at New Orleans; it missed Waterloo, but later went to Paris, remaining in occupation until 1817.

51st (2nd Yorkshire, West Riding or King's Own Light Infantry) Regiment

In 1770 the regiment was on Minorca, where John Moore joined it as an ensign. It stayed on the island until 1780, then went to Gibraltar. It was at Toulon in 1793 and Corsica in 1794, and remained there until 1798 when it returned to Gibraltar. It subsequently went to Portugal and from there to India and Ceylon. In 1807, after service in Kandy, it returned home; in 1808 it went to Spain and fought at Corunna. In May 1809 it was made a Light Infantry Corps, and served at Walcheren. In 1811 it joined the Peninsular Army. It was at Waterloo, went to Paris, and remained in occupation until 1816.

52nd (Oxfordshire) (Light Infantry) Regiment

After the War of Independence the regiment went to India and served against Tippoo Sahib, gaining the honour 'HINDOOSTAN'. Later it served in Ceylon, then returned to Britain where, reinforced by good volunteers, it was increased to two battalions. The 1st was at Quiberon, then at Cadiz. In January 1803 it was made a Light Infantry Corps, but standards were so exacting that many of the men were not considered suitable for the new rôle. They were transferred to a fresh battalion, which became the 96th. A new 2nd Battalion with adequate volunteer recruits was raised in 1804.

In 1807–8 the 1st was in Sicily, where NCOs helped train peasants for British service. In 1807 the 2nd was at Copenhagen and the 1st was with Moore in Sweden. The latter went to Portugal, followed by the 2nd Battalion; both were at Vimiero, and later at Corunna and Vigo respectively. The 2nd Battalion was next at Walcheren. The 1st returned to Portugal in 1809 and became part of the Light Division. The 2nd was

An officer's jacket of the 7th Royal Fusiliers, *c*. 1812; note that in this regiment the red and blue-faced sides of the lapels were both decorated with gold lace loops and white edge-piping. The turn-backs are edged with gold lace on a blue ground, and bear gold grenades on blue patches. A water-colour by H. Oakes-Jones shows an additional button, making two pairs in all, in each gold-laced rear pleat. The full dress headdress of the 7th was a bearskin cap with a gilt plate and a small black leather peak, a white plume on the left, and a red patch at the upper rear; this bore a badge comprising the crown over a garter containing a rose, in gold for officers and white for rank-and-file.

with Graham in northern Holland in 1813–14. The 1st Battalion was at Waterloo, and then in Paris, remaining in occupation until 1818. The 2nd was disbanded in 1816.

68th (Durham) (Light Infantry) Regiment

The regiment was on Gibraltar in 1786 and later went to the West Indies, where it remained until returning to the 'Rock' in 1796. In 1799 a second battalion was raised, but as the men were only 'short service' volunteers it was reduced to a single-battalion corps when returned to the West Indies in 1803. It remained in the Caribbean until 1806, suffering heavily from disease, and returned a mere token force. Supplemented by strong drafts from the Militia, it was converted to a Light Infantry Corps in 1808 and trained by de Rottenberg. It served at Walcheren and later joined the Peninsular Army in 1811, remaining until the end of the campaign and the subsequent capture of Bordeaux. It was in Ireland in 1815.

71st (Glasgow Highland Light Infantry) Regiment

Fraser's Highlanders, the old 71st, were disbanded after the War of Independence and the number in the Line was left vacant. The old 73rd, Macleod's, became the 71st (Highland) to fill the vacancy. It was in India 1790–91, with Baird at the Cape in 1800, went to Buenos Aires, and from thence to Portugal. It was at Vimiero and Corunna, and was made a Light Infantry Corps after its return. The 2nd Battalion, raised in 1803, remained a home service battalion. The 1st was

An important private soldier's jacket of a flank company of the 87th Regiment, *c*. 1812, which was in the collection of the French military painter Raymond Desvarreux. Of dull red cloth, it has green collar, cuffs and shoulder straps, and red wings. There is a red line woven into the white lace near one edge, falling at the outside of the pointed loops. The pewter buttons bear the Prince of Wales's feathers above his scroll above a harp above '87'.

at Walcheren and in 1810 was in Portugal, remaining in the Peninsula until the end of the war. It later served at Waterloo and went to Paris, remaining in occupation until 1818. The 2nd Battalion was disbanded in 1815. The title was altered and 'Glasgow' omitted in 1811.

85th (Bucks Volunteers Light Infantry) Regiment

Raised in 1778, it served for years in the West Indies. Many of its officers and men perished in

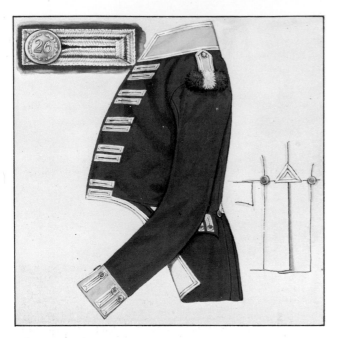

A private soldier's jacket of the 26th Regiment of the Peninsular War period, in the collection of the Baron Louis de Beaufort. It has a dull yellow collar, cuffs and shoulder straps, the latter terminating in extraordinary red/white/red tufts. The white lace has a dark blue stripe between two yellow stripes; the flat pewter buttons bear only the number, wreathed.

A private soldier's jacket of a battalion company of the 83rd Regiment, an excellent example of a Peninsular War period infantry jacket which was in the collection of the late Gen. Vanson. Dull red with yellow collar, cuffs and shoulder straps; white lace with a red and a green stripe; buttons bearing the number only. Note that the lace edging the turnbacks is brought forward along the front edge of the jacket, terminating just outside the bottom front loop.

storms at sea during its return to the UK. As a result it was disbanded, and re-formed in 1794 on the Duke of Buckingham's estates. In 1794 it was with the Duke of York in Flanders, and subsequently at Gibraltar, where it absorbed the remains of the 108th Regiment. It returned in 1799 to Holland, where a second battalion was raised.

The 1st occupied Madeira 1800–1801, then went to Jamaica where it remained until 1808. On its return to the UK it was made a Light Infantry Corps. It was at Walcheren, then in Portugal, where it suffered severely; it was repatriated in 1811. With a fresh officer establishment it returned to the Peninsula in 1813, and after the war sailed for America from the south of France. It fought at Bladensberg, Washington and New Orleans, suffering severe casualties at the latter. It returned to the UK in time for, but did not take part in, the Waterloo campaign. In August 1815 it received the title 'Duke of York's Light Infantry'.

90th (Perthshire Volunteers) Regiment

Soon after its formation in 1794 a second battalion was raised, but was presently drafted into the Marines. The regiment was at Quiberon and then went to Gibraltar. From 1798 it served on Minorca, and in 1801 in Egypt under Rowland Hill. After that campaign it went to Malta and from there returned to the UK. In 1804, while in Ireland, a further second battalion was raised, but this remained a home service battalion and was disbanded in 1817. In 1805 the 1st Battalion went to the West Indies and served on Antigua, Martinique, and Guadeloupe, remaining in occupation until 1814 when it was sent to Canada. It returned to Britain in 1815 and went to Belgium to join the army en route to Paris. It served in the Army of Occupation until 1816, then returned home.

The Rifle Corps

Baron de Rottenberg of the 60th Regiment wrote a special paper on the training of rifle units which influenced the thinking of Sir John Moore. In 1800 Coote Manningham published standing orders for his experimental corps under the title 'Regulations for the Rifle Corps formed at Blatchington Barracks under the command of Colonel Manningham'. His philosophy, similar to de Rottenberg's, was to dispense with the long-standing system of rigid and unthinking obedience to orders, and to replace it with what was for the time a novel form of discipline based on absolute trust between officer, NCO and soldier. The trust was to operate both ways, upwards and downwards in the chain of command, all ranks respecting each other.

Orders were expected to be given with moderation, bad language and blows being specifically forbidden: a 'new' pattern of training which gives some idea of the accepted methods used by Line infantry as a whole. Companies were carefully instructed to act on the principle that they could operate separately from, and be totally independent of, each other. Junior officers were equally divided between companies, and never

A beautifully preserved coatee worn by the commanding officer of the 2/42nd during the Peninsular War, and presented to the officers' mess of the 2nd Bn. The Black Watch in 1913 by W. A. Baird. It is of superfine scarlet cloth with dark blue facings and rich gold lace. On the turn-backs, and on the straps of the superb gold bullion epaulettes, may be seen the star of the Order of the Thistle; the same motif is cut into the buttons. (By permission The Black Watch Museum, courtesy G.A. Embleton)

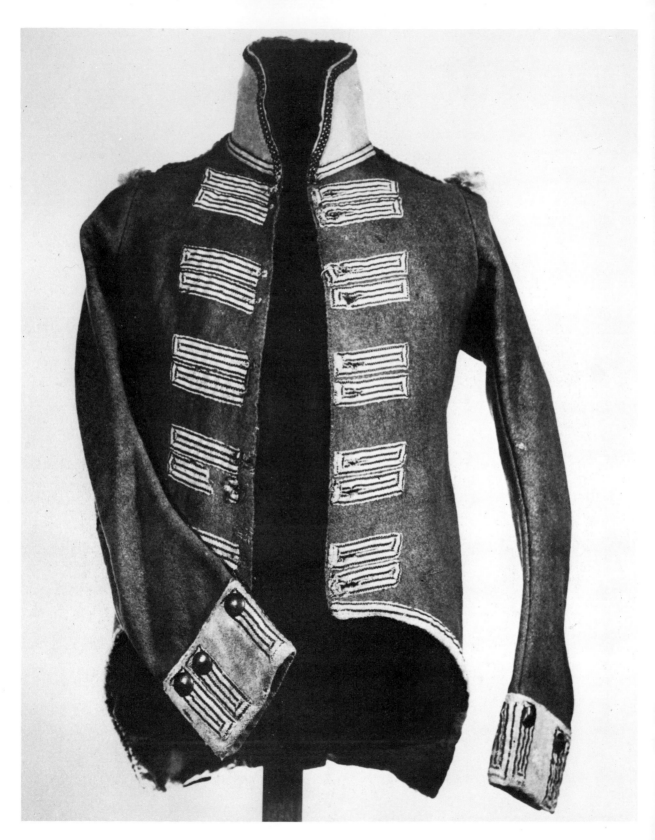

Dull red jacket, faced yellow, of a 9th Regiment private, *c.* 1815. Most of the lace has two black lines, now faded to brown; the curious black, white and brown collar lace seems to be a later addition. The remaining buttons do not seem to be original: they should be flat pewter with 'IX' in a scroll. Note drawn thread tufts at the end of the shoulder

10

straps. These photos show an excellent and rare example of the workmanship of soldier's jackets. (Photos J. Lorette, courtesy G. A. Embleton)

Front and back views of an unusual jacket of the Loyal Lancaster Volunteers, 1802–13, which shows some of the odd detail which appears on such garments. Note the eight pointed loops down the front, the broad strip of turned-back white lining brought around the front of the waistand and the distinctive vertical opening at the rear seam of the cuffs. (By permission Lancaster City Museum, courtesy G.A. Embleton)

exchanged from company to company. Consequently a feeling of 'family' was engendered, so that small groups of riflemen, divorced from the main body of their battalion or division, could feel a special trust, comradeship, and even friendship with their own officers and NCOs. In every half-platoon a soldier of merit was selected. These were the so-called 'chosen men' and when the NCOs were absent or wounded these men assumed responsibility for the squad. All corporals were promoted from among the 'chosen men'.

Each Company was divided into two equally-sized platoons, and these were again divided into halves. Officers and NCOs were allocated to each in proportion, and were never to be posted elsewhere unless at the express order of the battalion or company commander, or otherwise in extreme emergency. Within each squad riflemen picked comrades who were to be their permanent 'front-' or 'rear-rank' men. Their relative positions were never altered without the permission of the company commander. The three men trained, fought,

ate, and bivouacked together; as far as possible they were never parted, whether in barracks, quarters, or in the field. Corporals formed with chosen men, and buglers (used instead of drummers) formed with the odd men of any two squads. Messes were formed of about ten men, under the general direction of a corporal. There were also sergeants' and officers' messes.

Every company commander was able to offer prizes for the best shots in his command. First class marksmen were given green cockades. Others were classified as second- and third-class shots. In addition special awards were given for good conduct and long and meritorious service.

Moore's training of the Light Infantry and the 95th followed much the same principles. Men were taught to fight as 'thinking fighting men'; field exercises were made as realistic as possible, and were designed to bring out the best individual qualities in all ranks. They were taught to move swiftly, to march at ease, to bivouac by the roadside rather than spend time searching for billets, and to cook, launder and cobble as squads. Training involved specialised fieldcraft, skirmishing tactics, expertise in penetrating the enemy's lines, surprise in taking outposts, and the ability to act as reliable advance and rearguards.

In Coote Manningham's words: '. . . When time is to be gained, whether it be for the arrival

of troops destined to support the advance guards, to warn the army of the march and approach of the enemy, or to prevent surprise, it is the duty of the advanced guard neither to suffer its retreat to be cut off, nor its flanks turned, but to retire slowly, and in succession if possible, yielding but little ground at a time, keeping up constant fire and skirmishing, in order, by this method, to apprise the army of the enemy's movements . . . '

Officer of a battalion company of the 9th Regiment, from Goddard. Note the traditional Britannia badge displayed on the belt plate and the cap; on the belt plate it surmounts a label inscribed 'IX REGT', all mounted in silver. Goddard executed this plate in 1812, and shows the newly introduced high-fronted shako.

The Experimental Corps of Riflemen 1800–1802

In the spring of 1800 Col. Coote Manningham and Lt. Col. the Hon. William Stewart were ordered to use experience they had gained leading light troops in the West Indies, and their observations of Continental light troops on the Helder, to raise an Experimental Corps of Riflemen. Their first recruits were drawn from 13 regiments of the line (2/1st, 21st, 23rd, 25th, 27th, 29th, 49th, 69th, 71st, 72nd, 79th, 85th and 92nd). Each regiment provided one captain, one lieutenant, one ensign, two sergeants, one corporal, and 30 privates. In addition 12 active young recruits were drawn from 33 Fencible Regiments. They were sent to Blatchington Barracks, where they were formed into companies and issued with new dark green clothing. They were also issued with rifles, and during the summer that followed were trained in particular field exercises devised by Manningham. In August the same year they took part in their first action when they served with an expedition to the great arsenal at Ferrol. The mission as a whole was a failure, but the

13

The probably anomalous inclusion of the 1812 model shako does not detract from the splendidly spirited quality of this Peninsular War battle painting. At left, the grenadier company of an infantry battalion move into a village under fire, directed by a field officer in a bicorne hat.

riflemen learnt a great deal while covering the amphibious landings and disembarkation.

Back in Britain they learnt that they were to be disbanded, but soon afterwards were re-embodied and continued to train, gradually increasing in strength by the addition of volunteers from various Fencible and Volunteer regiments. In 1801 a detachment had the honour to serve as marksmen on Nelson's flagship during the bombardment of Copenhagen.

The 95th (Rifle) Regiment of Foot

In 1802 the Experimental Corps of Riflemen was brought into the Line as the 95th (Rifle) Regiment. In 1803 the battalion trained at Shorncliffe with the newly formed Light Infantry regiments, the 43rd and 51st. In 1805 a second battalion was raised at Canterbury, while the premier battalion was serving in Germany. In 1806 several companies accompanied Crauford to Buenos

Aires; the remainder went first to Copenhagen and later into Sweden with Moore.

The regiment was in Spain in 1808, fought at Vimiero, and later took part in the 1809 retreat on Vigo. It returned to the Peninsula in May 1809, when it formed part of Crauford's Brigade, which later became the famous Light Division. The 1/95th fought with Wellington in all the Peninsular battles until 1814 when it moved to northern Holland. It then went to Belgium and took part in the Waterloo campaign, later marching to Paris where it remained in occupation until 1813, when it returned to the United Kingdom.

In 1805 part of the 2nd Battalion took part in the storming of Montevideo. These companies later joined those of the 1st Battalion in the unsuccessful attack on Buenos Aires. The remainder of the 2nd Battalion served in the Copenhagen expedition of 1807; then went to Portugal and fought at Obidos, Relica and Vimiero. Subsequently they went to Walcheren. The 2nd Battalion went back to the Peninsula in 1810 and joined the 1st Battalion in the Light Division during 1811–14. Part was in Holland in 1814, and in 1815 this battalion also served at Waterloo, went to Paris, and returned home in 1816.

A third battalion was raised in 1809; part went to Cadiz in 1810 and later fought at Barossa. This section later joined Wellington and served out the Peninsular campaign with the 1st and 2nd Battalions. Elements went to Stralsund in 1813, and later to Holland. After the close of the Peninsular War five companies of the 3rd Battalion went to America and fought with Pakenham at New Orleans; other companies were attached to the 2nd, went to Belgium and served at Waterloo, later being rejoined by the remainder of the battalion returning from America.

Officer and private of the 85th Light Infantry, c. 1810, by P.W. Reynolds; the facings are yellow, the officer's 'metal' silver. Note that this officer wears the same shako as his men, and the narrow light infantry sash which terminated in long cords and 'bell rope' tassels.

A pen and ink sketch by Capt. Jones, one of a set depicting incidents during the battle of Waterloo, allegedly drawn on the actual battlefield. Here Wellington is spurring up to Maitland's Foot Guards to order them into action against the advancing French Imperial Guard at the climax of the battle. It was at this moment that he gave the order 'Now, Maitland! Now's your time!'—rather than the more theatrical, and apocryphal, 'Up, Guards, and at 'em!'

The 5th Battalion, 60th (Royal American) Regiment

The fifth battalion was added to the regiment by Act of Parliament on 30 December 1797: 'An Act to enable His Majesty to Grant Commissions to a certain number of foreign Protestants who have served abroad as Officers or Engineers' . . . It originally consisted of 1,000 men, including foreign troops in His Majesty's pay, or other foreigners who volunteered to serve. The number of officers in the battalion was ordered not to exceed 50 and the number of foreign engineers not to exceed 20. None of the foreign officers were permitted to serve anywhere else but in America; but in 1804 a further Act was passed authorising 10,000 foreign troops to serve in the United Kingdom. Lt. Gen. Baron de Rottenberg was appointed colonel, and the 5/60th was formed at Cowes, Isle of Wight.

Four hundred of the earliest recruits were from Hompesch's Mounted Riflemen. The battalion was ordered to be dressed in green and to carry 'rifle-bags' of brown leather instead of knapsacks. The NCOs and men, and no doubt the officers, were allowed to wear moustaches, which all added to their 'foreign' appearance.

In 1798 the battalion was moved to Ireland, and later returned to Cowes and from there to the

A mounted field officer of an infantry battalion, left, with a member of the brigade staff. Note the shape of the saddle-cloth, which was in regimental facing colour with an edging of regimental officers' lace. After R. Simpkin.

including Dutch, Swiss and Hungarians. Of the 800 rank and file, 640 were called 'light infantry' while the remainder were called 'riflemen'.

The 8th Battalion was formed at Lisbon in 1813, and there were projections to raise 9th and even 10th Battalions, but these do not appear to have been anything more than 'paper' units.

Six battalions were disbanded after the peace of 1815. Drafts of the 8th went to the 5th; the remainder were sent home. The 7th was disbanded at Halifax in 1817, and the elements drafted to the 2nd and 3rd Battalions. The 6th Battalion was disbanded at Portsmouth in 1818 and the men went into the 3rd; the 5th was disbanded at the Isle of Wight in 1818 and its NCOs and men were drafted into the 2nd, which was at Quebec. The latter was then retitled the 'Rifle Battalion' and the 3rd the 'Light Infantry'.

Finally the old 1st and 4th Battalions were disbanded, and drafted into the 2nd. The 2nd Battalion was then retitled the 1st (Rifle) Battalion and the 3rd became the 2nd (Light Infantry) Battalion. The regiment did not become a totally British unit until 1824.

West Indies, where it was reinforced by 33 officers and 600 NCOs and men from Lowenstein's Chasseurs. It later went to South America, and from there to Canada. In 1805 the battalion returned to England and the following year received an additional 44 officers, 22 sergeants and 800 rank and file. It then went to Ireland. In June 1808 the battalion embarked for Portugal. It fought during 1808–14 in most major actions of the Peninsular War, its companies normally operating dispersed in ones and twos, to give the various Line brigades a skirmishing capability: see Men-at-Arms 114, p. 13.

The 6th, 7th and 8th Battalions 60th (Royal American) Regiment
In 1799 two further battalions were raised. The 6th comprised nearly all Germans, and the 7th either Germans or other former prisoners-of-war

The Highland Regiments

Lord Forbes of Culloden has been given credit for first considering forming regiments from various existing independent companies of Highlanders. They were increased by the addition of a further four companies in 1739 and were all then embodied as the 43rd Regiment, renumbered the 42nd in 1749, and by July 1758 granted the title 42nd (Royal Highland) Regiment of Infantry. Between then and 1800 some 29 Highland Regiments were raised, ranging from the 77th (Montgomery's) in 1757, to the 133rd raised and disbanded in 1794, besides a long list of first-class Fencible Regiments, many of which provided recruits for the surviving corps.

42nd Royal Highland (The Black Watch) Regiment
After a distinguished record in the War of Independence the 1st Battalion returned to the

United Kingdom. It was with the Duke of York in the Low Countries, then returned to the West Indies, serving at St Vincent and St Lucia, where it absorbed survivors of the 79th. It took part in the capture of Minorca in 1798, and was then at Cadiz and later on Malta before taking part in the Egyptian campaign In 1805 it was at Gibraltar, remaining there until 1808 when it went to Portugal, fighting at Rolica and Vimiero. It was with Moore at Corunna, and subsequently at Walcheren. In 1812 it returned to the Peninsula and served there until the end of the campaign. It later fought at Waterloo and was in occupation in Paris. The 2nd Battalion was in India in 1781, when it was reconstituted as the 73rd Regiment. A further 2nd Battalion was raised in 1803 and went to Spain, but returned home in 1812, relieved by the 1st. In remained in the UK until 1814 when it was disbanded.

72nd (formerly the 78th) (Duke of Albany's Own Highlanders) Regiment

After the Peace of 1783 the old 78th (Fraser's) was renumbered the 72nd. It served in India against Tippoo Sahib and returned home in 1798. In 1804 a second battalion was formed, but remained a home service battalion until disbandment in 1814. The regiment was at the Cape in 1805 and remained in South Africa for five years, breaking service to form part of the force sent to Mauritius, but returned to South Africa and stayed at the Cape until 1815.

In this reconstruction of the 85th Light Infantry skirmishing in the Peninsula, R. Simpkin has elected to show the officer wearing a cylindrical shako with green cap lines while the rank and file, including the bugler, wear similarly-decorated 'Waterloo' shakos. The officer has a buttoned-over jacket, heavily plated shoulder wings, and overalls with leather booting.

73rd (Perthshire) Regiment

In 1786 the former 2nd Battalion of the 42nd was reconstituted as the 73rd Foot. It served against Tippoo Sahib in 1790–91, was in Ceylon in 1795, and fought at the siege of Seringapatam in 1799. It then fought against the Polygars, returning home in 1806. A year later it re-embarked for New South Wales, serving there and in Tasmania until 1814. The 2nd Battalion, raised in 1809, fought with Gibbs at Stralsund and later at Göhrde in Hanover, and in northern Holland. It joined Wellington for Waterloo and later went to Paris, returning home at the end of the year. NB: The 73rd discontinued Highland dress in 1809.[1]

[1]The 74th Regiment embarked for India in 1788, and on arrival in Madras the kilt was discontinued in favour of white linen pantaloons. Leaving India in 1805, and arriving back in Britain in February 1806, the regiment resumed full Highland dress. In 1809 both the 74th and 75th discontinued Highland dress finally, as it was considered '. . . an impediment to recruitment'.

78th (Highland) (Ross-shire Buffs) Regiment

Raised in 1793, it was permitted to add 'Ross-shire Buffs' to its title, and raised a second battalion a year later.

The 1st served in Holland, 1794–95, and in the Vendee. The 2nd went to South Africa, where it was joined by the 1st in 1796. There the battalions were amalgamated and went on to India, gaining great honour at Assaye. A special honorary third Colour was awarded for this action by the Honourable East India Company.

A further 2nd Battalion was later raised and went to Sicily, taking part in the campaign in Calabria. It was at Maida, and then went to Egypt. In 1809 it went to India, where it merged with the 1st; the much-reduced regiment returned to Scotland, where it stayed until 1813. Recruited to strength, it went with Graham to Holland in 1813–14, serving alongside Prussian infantry. It remained in the Low Countries; formed the garrison of Brussels until June 1815, and then the garrison of Nieuport; and afterwards returned to Scotland. It went to Java in 1811 and then to India, where it remained until 1817.

79th (Cameron Highlanders) Regiment

Raised by Alan Cameron of Erracht in 1793, it joined the Duke of York in the Low Countries in 1794. It was later sent to the West Indies and was ravaged by yellow fever and malaria. The few surviving officers were sent home and the NCOs and men were absorbed into the 42nd. A fresh battalion was recruited and posted to the Channel Islands, and from there to Holland. In 1801 it went to Egypt and from there to Minorca. A second battalion had meanwhile been raised. The 1st was at Copenhagen in 1807, returned to Egypt in 1808, and then went to Portugal. It was at Corunna and then went to Walcheren. It subsequently returned to the Peninsula and fought during the remainder of the campaign. From southern France the 1st Battalion proceeded to Ireland, and thence to Belgium and the Waterloo campaign. It went to Paris and remained in occupation until 1818. The 2nd Battalion remained in Scotland until disbandment in 1814.

91st (Argyllshire) Regiment

The regiment served at the Cape from 1796 until 1802 and then returned to the United Kingdom. In 1803 a second battalion was raised. The 1st served in Portugal in 1808, fighting at Rolica and Vimiero, and was at Corunna. It subsequently went to Walcheren, and then took part in the 1813–14 Peninsular campaign. It then went to the Mediterranean theatre, where it remained until after Waterloo.

The 2nd Battalion went to Mecklenberg in 1813 and from there to Holland and later Belgium. It was in reserve at Huy during the Waterloo campaign, but subsequently went to France, returning home in 1816 when it was disbanded. NB: It was ordered to cease wearing Highland dress in 1809.

92nd (Gordon Highlanders) Regiment

Raised in 1794 as the 100th, it was stationed for some time at Gibraltar and subsequently went to Corsica, a detachment serving on Elba. The battalion returned to the United Kingdom in 1798 and served in Ireland. In 1798 the regiment was renumbered the 92nd, and went to Holland. It served at Quiberon, Ferrol and Cadiz and in 1801 went to Egypt. The first battalion was at

Copenhagen in 1807, then in Sweden, and subsequently in Portugal. It was with Moore at Corunna, and then went to Walcheren. It returned to Spain, fought in most major engagements until the war finished and was at Waterloo. It went to Paris, and returned home in 1816. The 2nd Battalion was a home service unit, disbanded in 1814.

93rd (Sutherland Highlanders) Regiment

Raised in 1800 in the Sutherland and Ross areas, mostly from recruits provided by good Fencible

P.W. Reynolds's reconstruction of the Line infantry uniform worn at Waterloo, including the oilskin shako cover shown by Dighton and mentioned by the Rev. Gleig.

regiments, it first served in the Channel Islands. It later went to the Cape with Baird, stayed in South Africa until 1814, and then returned to the United Kingdom. It went to America with Pakenham and fought at New Orleans, where it suffered heavy casualties. The battalion then returned to Ireland where it remained until 1815. A second battalion, raised in 1814, served in Newfoundland until 1815, when it returned home and was disbanded.

Other Units

Garrison, Reserve and Veteran Battalions and Companies

Before 1802 there were Invalid Corps performing garrison duties throughout the United Kingdom. By 1803 these units were used to create Garrison Battalions, and in 1804 were re-titled Royal Veteran Battalions. Originally seven battalions each of ten companies were formed, but six further battalions were raised before the end of the Napoleonic Wars. Some served overseas; the 1st saw service on Gibraltar and later in Holland, and others served in New South Wales, Madeira and Canada. The 13th, later renumbered the 7th Battalion, was a strong unit of ten companies totalling about 1,000 rank and file and served as the garrison at Lisbon. It was disbanded in 1816, but not before it was granted the battle honour 'Peninsula'.

In 1803, 16 'Battalions of Reserve' were raised for service in the United Kingdom and the Channel Islands, but the following year they were re-titled Garrison Battalions. The service was re-organised in 1805, and re-embodied as the 1st, 2nd and 3rd Garrison Battalions. Six further battalions were raised in 1806.

In June 1815 eight battalions known as Royal Veterans were raised from Chelsea Pensioners, but were disbanded the following year. Overseas there was a similar development. From 1803 to 1808 two companies known as the European Garrison Companies were raised in Jamaica and Barbados from white soldiers no longer fit for active duty. They were disbanded in 1814 and 1817. Negro soldiers from West India regiments

no longer fit for active service were formed into two Black Garrison Companies in 1813, but both units were disbanded four years later. There was a Veteran Company at the Cape of Good Hope between 1813 and the end of the Napoleonic Wars, and a Veteran Company in New South Wales between 1810 and 1815.

The Garrison Company of the King's German Legion was formed in 1805 for veterans of the force no longer fit for active service. On 8 December 1812 this company was incorporated into the 1st Foreign Veteran Battalion and attached to the Legion. This unit initially comprised four companies, of which the Garrison Company was one, and was later expanded to six, one being in Hanover. The unit was disbanded in Hanover in 1816.

Sergeant and private of the 1801 period, from a painting by Richard Simpkin; note the NCO's 9ft. pike, the powdered and queued hair, and the breeches and gaiters.

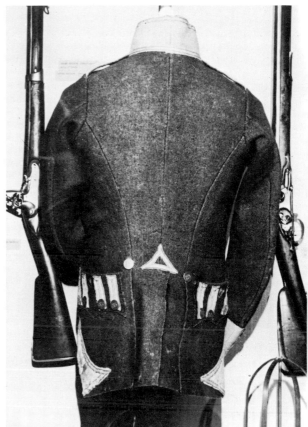

The West India Regiments

Brig. Gen. Hislop and Major Robert Malcolm of the 41st Regiment are credited with raising the first regular black regiments, although nearly all the Caribbean Islands had their embodied negro Ranger units. While serving as Town Major of St Pierre-Martinique, Malcolm raised a unit known as 'Malcolm's Corps', or 'Malcolm's Corps of Rangers'. He was killed in action in 1796 but his unit, highly thought of by that time, survived and was subsequently amalgamated with the equally distinguished 'Black Carolina Corps'. In 1795 it was renamed 'Whyte's Regiment', and later became the 1st West India Regiment. A second corps, formerly 'Myer's St Vincent Rangers', became the 2nd West India Regiment.

The 3rd and 4th Regiments were raised in 1795 and served until 1817, when they were disbanded. The 5th and 6th, raised in 1798, were also disbanded in 1817, but a 7th Regiment raised about the same time was disbanded in 1802.

The 8th, a small unit of only six companies, was an unsatisfactory corps and was broken up

Front and rear of a private's jacket of the 83rd Regiment, *c.* 1808–14. Note the hook-and-eye front fastening; the sturdy quality of the coarse red cloth; and, particularly, the pocket detail. The simulated flaps are sewn down along the bottom and side edges but are open at the top, the opening being closed by an additional small button set centrally. A loop of lace is missing from each cuff; the flat pewter buttons bear a raised '83' only; and the shoulders have neither wings nor tufts. **(National Army Museum)**

after a mutiny. The 9th to 12th Regiments were raised in 1798, the former from Drualt's 'Guadelope Rangers' and the 10th from De Soter's 'Royal Island Rangers'. The 11th became the 8th after the mutiny, the 9th was disbanded in 1813, and the 10th was disbanded in 1802. The 11th and 12th were disbanded in 1803. Elements of the 7th to 12th were drafted to the senior regiments.

It was the appalling losses from yellow fever and malaria which convinced Horse Guards of the need to recruit blacks. It was felt that negro soldiers could safely carry out many of the labouring and fatigue duties which broke the health of so many white troops in the tropics. Rank and

continued on page 24

Regimental Distinctions

The details are from Hamilton Smith's charts of 1812; it will be noted that in a few cases these differ from those quoted in MAA 114 from De Bosset's 1803 charts, and that different proofs of Hamilton Smith's work vary in the design of the men's lace for many regiments. The columns show number and title of regiment (*NB*: in several cases no territorial designation was awarded); facing colour; colour of officer's lace and buttons; shape and spacing of lace loops on men's coats; and pattern in men's lace. Abbreviations are, for officers' lace, 'G' = gold, 'S' = silver. Loop shape and spacing is indicated e.g. 'S1' = square-ended loops arranged evenly, 'B2' = bastion-formed loops arranged in pairs, 'P3' = pointed loops arranged in threes. Changes are given as e.g. '1812–' = 'from 1812 onwards.'

No. & title	Facings	Officers' lace	Loop shape, spacing	Men's lace pattern
1st, Royal Scots	Blue	G	S2 (B1, 1812–)	Double blue worm
2nd, Queen's Royal	Blue	S	S1	Blue stripe
3rd, East Kent, or (Old) Buffs	Buff	S	S2	Yellow, black & red stripes
4th, King's Own	Blue	G	B1	Blue stripe
5th, Northumberland	Gosling green	S	B1	Two red stripes
6th, 1st Warwickshire	Yellow	S	S2	Yellow & red stripes
7th, The Royal Fusiliers	Blue	G	S1	Blue stripe
8th, King's	Blue	G	S1	Blue & yellow stripes
9th, E. Norfolk	Yellow	S	S2	Two black or blue stripes
10th, N. Lincolnshire	Yellow	S	S1	Blue stripe
11th, N. Devonshire	Deep green	S	B2	Two red & two green stripes
12th, E. Suffolk	Yellow	G	B2	Yellow, crimson red & black stripes
13th, 1st Somersetshire	Yellow	S	S2	Red stripe
14th, Buckinghamshire	Buff	S	S2	Red & black worms; or blue & red worms and buff stripe
15th, Yorkshire (East Riding)	Yellow	S	S2	Yellow/black worm and red stripe
16th, Bedfordshire	Yellow	S	S1	Crimson red stripe
17th, Leicestershire	White	S	S2	Blue, red & blue stripes; or two blue, one yellow stripes
18th, Royal Irish	Blue	G	S2	Blue stripe
19th, 1st Yorkshire (North Riding)	Green	G	S2	Red, green & red stripes; 1815–, black worm on green cloth
20th, East Devonshire	Yellow	S	S2	Red & black stripes
21st, Royal North British Fusiliers	Blue	G	S2	Blue stripe
22nd, Cheshire	Buff	G	B2	Blue & red stripes
23rd, Royal Welsh Fusiliers	Blue	G	B1	Red, blue & yellow stripes
24th, Warwickshire	Green	S	S2	Red & green stripes
25th, King's Own Borderers	Blue	G	B1	Blue, red & yellow stripes; or red & yellow only
26th, Cameronian	Yellow	S	S2	Red, yellow, blue, yellow & red stripes; or one blue, two yellow stripes

No. & title	Facings	Officers' lace	Loop shape, spacing	Men's lace pattern
61st, South Gloucestershire	Buff	S	S1	Blue stripe
62nd, Wiltshire	Buff	S	S2	Blue, straw yellow & blue stripes
63rd, West Suffolk	Deep green	S	S2	Thin dark green stripe
64th, 2nd Staffordshire	Black	S	S2	Black and red stripes
65th, 2nd Yorkshire (North Riding)	White	G	S2	Red & yellow worm & black stripe; or red & black worm & black stripe. (1814–) two black stripes
66th, Berkshire	Gosling green	S	S1	Crimson red & green stripes
67th, South Hampshire	Yellow	S	S2	Purplish red & green stripes
68th, Durham	Bottle green	S	S2	Red & green stripes; or yellow & black stripes
69th, South Lincolnshire	Green	G	S2	Green, red & green stripes
70th, Glasgow Lowland	Black	G	S1	Black stripe or worm
71st, Highland Light Infantry	Buff	S	S1	Red stripe
72nd, Highland	Yellow	S	B1	Greenish-blue stripe
73rd, Highland	Green	G	B1	Red stripe
74th, Highland	White	G	S1	Red stripe
75th, Highland	Yellow	S	S2	Two yellow & one red stripes
76th	Red	S	S2	Black or dark blue stripe
77th, East Middlesex	Yellow	S	S1	Red & yellow stripes; or black stripe
78th, Highland (Ross-shire Buffs)	Buff	G	B1	Green stripe
79th, Cameron Highlanders	Dark green	G	S2	Red, yellow & red stripes
80th, Staffordshire Volunteers	Yellow	G	S2	Black, red & black stripes; or two red & one black stripes
81st	Buff	S	S2	Red & green stripes
82nd, Prince of Wales's Volunteers	Yellow	S	B2	Black or blue stripe
83rd	Yellow	G	S2	Red & green stripes
84th, York and Lancaster	Yellow	S	S2	Scarlet, blue & scarlet stripes; or two scarlet stripes
85th, Bucks Volunteers	Yellow	S	S2	Red 'battlement' figure & blue stripe; or two red worms & two black stripes
86th, Royal County Down	Blue	S	S2	Blue, two red, blue stripes
87th, Prince of Wales's Own Irish	Green	G	S2	Red stripe
88th, Connaught Rangers	Yellow	S	S2	Blue, red & yellow stripes; or two red & one yellow stripes

Regiment	Facing			Lace
27th, Inniskilling	Buff	G	S1	Blue & red stripes
28th, North Gloucestershire	Yellow	S	S2	One black, two yellow stripes; or two black, one yellow stripes
29th, Worcestershire	Yellow	S	P2	Yellow, two black, yellow stripes; or two blue, one yellow stripes
30th, Cambridgeshire	Yellow	S	B1	Light blue stripe
31st, Huntingdonshire	Buff	S	S1	Red stripe; or blue & yellow worm
32nd, Cornwall	White	G	S2	Red stripe
33rd, 1st Yorkshire (West Riding)	Red	S	B2	Red stripe
34th, Cumberland	Yellow	S	S2	Red stripe, blue & yellow worm
35th, Sussex	Orange	S	S2	Blue, yellow & red stripes
36th, Herefordshire	Gosling green	G	S2	Green & red stripes
37th, North Hampshire	Yellow	S	S2	Yellow & red stripes; or plain lace
38th, 1st Staffordshire	Yellow	S	S1	Red, yellow & red stripes
39th, Dorsetshire	Pea green	G	S2	Light green stripe
40th, 2nd Somersetshire	Buff	G	S2	Red & black stripes
41st	Red	S	B1	Black stripe
42nd, Royal Highland	Blue	G	B1	Red stripe
43rd, Monmouthshire	White	S	S2	Black & red stripes
44th, East Essex	Yellow	S	S1	Black, yellow & black stripes
45th, Nottinghamshire	Dark green	S	B2	Green stripe
46th, South Devonshire	Pale yellow	S	S2	Red & purple stripes or worms
47th, Lancashire	White	S	S2	Black, red & black stripes
48th, Northamptonshire	Buff	G	S2	Black & red stripes
49th, Hertfordshire	Green	G	B1	Two red & one green stripes
50th, West Kent	Black	G	S2	Red stripe
51st, 2nd Yorkshire (West Riding)	Grass green	G	S2 (P2?)	Green worm or stripe
52nd, Oxfordshire	Buff	S	S2	Black, red & buff stripes; or red worm, orange stripe
53rd, Shropshire	Red	G	S2	Red stripe
54th, West Norfolk	Green	S	S2	Green stripe
55th, Westmoreland	Green	G	S2	Two green stripes
56th, West Essex	Purple	S	S2	Light red stripe
57th, West Middlesex	Yellow	G	S1	Black stripe
58th, Rutlandshire	Black	G	S1	Red stripe
59th, 2nd Nottinghamshire	White	G	B1	Two blue stripes
60th, Royal American	Blue	S	S2	Two blue stripes

Regiment	Facing			Lace
89th	Black	G	S2	Red stripe; or red & blue stripes
90th, Perthshire Volunteers	Buff	G	S2	Blue & buff-yellow stripes
91st	Yellow	S	S2	Two yellow stripes; or black stripe & black worm
92nd, Gordon Highlanders	Yellow	S	S2	Dark blue or black stripe
93rd	Yellow	S	B2 (P2?)	Red stripe; or yellow stripe or worm
94th	Green	G	S2	Green & red stripes
95th Rifles	Black	None indicated	None	None
96th	Buff	S	S2	Blue, yellow & red stripes
97th, Queen's Own	Blue	S	S2	Red & blue stripes
98th	Buff	S	S1	Red, blue, red & blue stripes
99th, Prince of Wales's Tipperary	Pale yellow	None indicated	S1	Yellow stripe
100th, HRH the Prince Regent's County of Dublin	Deep yellow	None indicated	S2	Blue, red, blue & red stripes
101st, Duke of York's Irish	White	None indicated	S2	Blue stripe
102nd	Yellow	S	S2	Yellow & blue stripes
103rd	White	None indicated	S1	Blue & red stripes
104th	Buff	None indicated	S2	Blue, yellow & red stripes
1st West India (NB: Half-lapels for WI Regts.)	White	S	S2	Blue or black stripe
2nd West India	Yellow	G	S2	Yellow & purplish-blue stripes
3rd West India	Yellow	S	S2	Black stripe
4th West India	Yellow	S	S1	Yellow, blue & yellow stripes
5th West India	Green	G	S1	Plain lace
6th West India	Yellow	S	S1	Black or blue stripe
7th West India	Yellow	S	S1	Brown, blue & yellow stripes
8th West India	Grey	S	S1	Red, yellow & black stripes
9th West India	Yellow	None indicated	S1	Two blue & one yellow stripes
10th West India	Buff	None indicated	S1	Scarlet & black stripes
11th West India	Green	None indicated	S1	Green edge stripe
12th West India	Buff	None indicated	S1	Scarlet stripe, black edge
King's German Legion Line Bns.	Blue	G	S2	Red stripe
Garrison Regts.	Blue	G	S1	Blue stripe

file were originally recruited from plantation slaves or Creole freedmen on the islands, but later regiments were almost entirely recruited in Africa, mainly from Ibos, Fantis, Coramantees and Angolas. Officers were white, and mostly British, although there were some Dutch and émigrés. Their quality was poor and there was a great deal of absenteeism. At one time only officers who had come bottom of their classes at Academies were posted to West India regiments. Senior NCOs were originally all European, but by 1815 most were coloured West Indians or Africans. From 1812 there was a permanent recruiting office in the Sierra Leone.

West India regiments fought with great distinction during the Napoleonic Wars and gained the honours 'Dominica', 'Martinique' and 'Guadelope'. Two regiments, the 1st and 5th, fought with Pakenham at New Orleans in 1814.

The King's German Legion

In July 1803 Lt. Col. von der Decken was granted a Royal Warrant to raise a corps of Hanoverians for the British service. Lymington in Hampshire was chosen as the depôt, and passage of candidates was arranged via Heligoland and Holstein. Although the French made strenuous efforts to curb any exodus of men, by the end of the year much progress had been made. The original concept had been for a limited force, but a legion of all arms now seemed possible. Recruitment proved so popular that nearly all the original entrants were Hanoverians, although Poles, Hungarians and Dutchmen from the prison hulks were sometimes admitted. Recruits usually enlisted for ten years, never less than seven. They had to be 5ft. 3ins. tall, but youths of 5ft. 2ins. with a potential for growth were encouraged. The maximum age for enlistment was 40 years. Officers and men took allegance to King George, and swore to serve where required subject to British Articles of War.

The first elements to be formed were the Light Infantry battalions, the first commanded by Carl von Alten and the second by Colin Halkett. The original establishment of these battalions was as follows, but was later amended to accommodate normal company strength: one lieutenant-colonel; one (later two) majors; six captains; six lieutenants; six ensigns; one adjutant; one paymaster; one surgeon; one (later two) assistant surgeons; one sergeant major; one quartermaster sergeant; one armourer sergeant; 24 sergeants; 24 corporals; 12 buglers; one pioneer and 450 soldiers. They were referred to by their German titles.

The pioneers wore leather aprons, carried shovels, billhooks, saws, axes or hatchets, and one of their number was usually a corporal. The buglers ('Hornists') were similarly led by a 'Stabshornist'. The battalions were initially to have ten companies, but in practice mostly had eight, and a sharpshooter half-company led by a subaltern with two sergeants, two corporals, a bugler and 52 men, all selected marksmen armed with rifles. The remainder of the companies were armed with the musket.

The raising of Line battalions followed; the establishment was to be the same except that drummers were included instead of buglers, and there was a drum major ('Bataillontambour'). Line battalions had grenadier companies, and sharpshooters, with buglers instead of drummers.

In early winter 1805 the Legion was in Hanover, where it remained until recruitment was considered complete, including eight Line battalions. The Colonel-in-Chief was Prince Adolphus Frederick, Duke of Cambridge, who was also Colonel of the Hanoverian Guard Battalion and the 1st Line Battalion. The Adjutant-General was Colonel von der Decken and his deputy Colonel von Linsingen. In February 1806 the Light and Line battalions were commanded as follows:

    1st Light Bn. Col. C. von Alten
    2nd Light Bn. Col. Colin Halkett
    1st Line Bn. Col. von Ompteda
    2nd Line Bn. Col. von Barsse
    3rd Line Bn. Col. Heinrich von Hinüber
    4th Line Bn. Col. E.L. von Simmern
    5th Line Bn. Col. G. von Drieberg
    6th Line Bn. Col. A. von Honstedt
    7th Line Bn. Col. F. von Drechsel
    8th Line Bn. Col. Peter von Plat

A Depôt Company was formed in November 1803, the Independent Garrison Company in 1805. Until 1811, in the Peninsula, all Line and

5th and 6th Bns., 60th Regiment:
1. Private, 5th Bn.;1797
2. Officer, 5th Bn.; 1799
3. Private, 6th Bn.; 1799

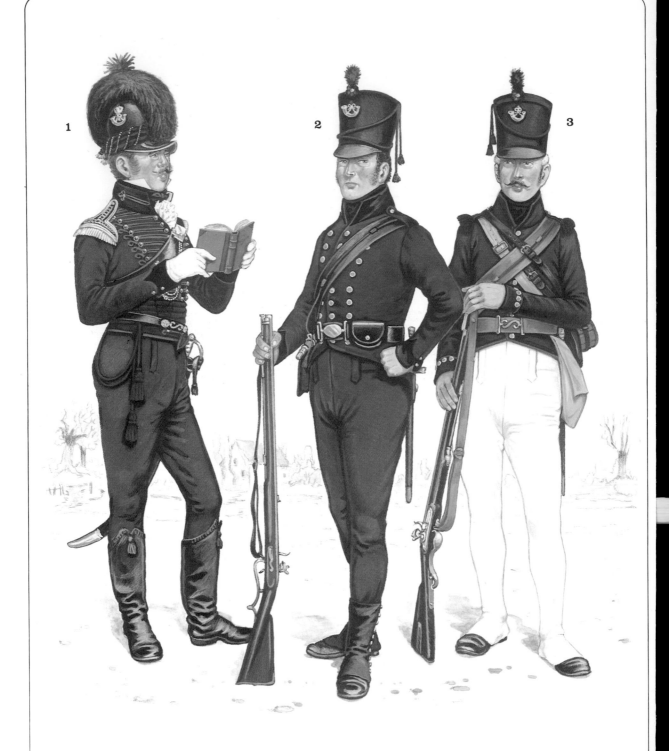

Experimental Corps of Riflemen and rifle companies of 60th Regt.:
1. Officer, Experimental Corps of Riflemen; 1800
2. Rifleman, Experimental Corps of Riflemen; 1800
3. Corporal, Rifle Company, 2nd Bn., 60th Regt.; 1800

The Light Infantry:
1. Officer, 43rd Regt.; 1812
2. Sergeant, 52nd Regt.; 1812
3. Private, 71st Regt.; 1812

C

95th Rifles:
1. Officer, 95th Regt.; 1811
2. Rifleman, 95th Regt.; 1811
3. Sergeant, 95th Regt.; 1811

D

The Highland Regiments:
1. Officer, Grenadier Company, 92nd Regt. (Gordon Highlanders); 1812
2. Sergeant, Light Coy., 79th Regt. (Cameron Highlanders); 1815
3. Private, Bn. Coy., 42nd (Royal Highland) Regt.; 1815

E

West India Regts. and 93rd Highlanders:
1. Sergeant, Grenadier Coy., 93rd Foot; 1812
2. Private, 5th West India Regt.; 1812
3. Officer, 1st West India Regt.; 1812

Light Bns., King's German Legion:
1. Sergeant, Sharpshooters, 2nd Light Bn., KGL; 1815
2. Officer, 2nd Light Bn., KGL; 1815
3. Private, 1st Light Bn., KGL; 1815

Line Bns., King's German Legion:
1. Sergeant, Sharpshooters, Light Coy., 3rd Line Bn., KGL; 1815
2. Officer, Grenadier Coy., 1st Line Bn., KGL; 1815
3. Private, Light Coy., 2nd Line Bn., KGL; 1815

H

Light battalion sharpshooters were massed in a battalion called the 'Scharfschützenkorps', but later those of the Light battalions returned to their units.

The Legion's service included campaigns in Germany 1805–06, the Baltic 1807, the Mediterranean and Sicily 1808–11, the Peninsula 1808–14, Walcheren 1809, Italy 1814, North Germany 1813–14 and Waterloo 1815. *Battle Honours*: Both Light battalions: 'Burgos'; 1st, 2nd, 4th and 5th Line battalions: 'Peninsula' and 'Waterloo'; 6th and 7th Line battalions: 'Peninsula'.

The Plates

A: 5th and 6th Bns., 60th Regiment
A1: Private, 5th Bn., 60th Regt., 1797
A2: Officer, 5th Bn., 60th Regt., 1799
A3: Private, 6th Bn., 60th Regt., 1799

Charles Hamilton Smith, who served on the Staff in the West Indies, made two small watercolours of riflemen of the 5th and 6th Bns., 60th Regt., in the uniforms worn in the last few years of the 18th century. These drawings, and the plate in the regimental history, are the sources for A1 and A3.

Maj. Gen. Astley Terry described the uniform of officers of the 5th Bn. from a portrait of an officer of the corps named Wollf: '... *a green jacket with scarlet facings, black braiding, and three rows of silver buttons in front* [NB: There is a portrait of Lt. Col. Crauford of the same period which shows a quite plain jacket. This is thought to be either an undress coat, or the uniform of a Hompesch regiment], *a crimson barrelled sash and green pantaloons with Hessian boots for full dress, in undress blue-grey trousers without stripes were worn, a black pouch belt with a silver [Maltese Cross] plate, whistle and chain. The sword was curved with a black leather scabbard and gilt mounts and was worn on slings, from a black waistbelt. The headdress was a black leather cap-helmet with a bearskin crest, green feather out of a scarlet rosette, the latter presumably an innovation of the Swiss Baron de Rottenberg ...*'

Note that both battalions wore green, although the 5th had red facings while the jacket of the

Universal brass plate worn on the 1801–12 shakos. Many regiments had their own 'ancient badges' struck in the centre of the garter in place of the Royal Cypher; grenadiers had a flaming grenade above the crown or beneath the Royal badge, and other regiments had their numbers either in the central garter, at the 'shoulders', or on each side of the Royal badge. (National Army Museum)

6th was plain green 'feathered' (edged) red. According to the Regimental Chronicle only the 5th Bn. were permitted moustaches. The battalions were issued with Prussian rifles, part of a large purchase and some of indifferent quality, but subsequently received the Baker.

A list of belongings of Lt. Col. Fitzgerald of the 5th Bn. was recorded in 1814, as follows: '*A green full trimmed jacket with Russia* [braid] *fronts, three sets of ball buttons, scarlet collar and cuffs. A green pelisse with sable fur, "Royal" cord breasts and full trimmed. A long blue pelisse, no fur. Green waist-*

coat, *full trimmed and a full dress waistcoat, silver braided. Blue overalls. Blue ornamented pantaloons. Full dress white pantaloons full trimmed. Steel [mounted] sword with a black leather scabbard and black belt with plated furniture. Green sash with scarlet barrels. Black pouch belt with a silver buglehorn on the lid. A cap with a tapered crown nine inches high, square peak, black silk lines twice round, two tassels, silver bugle.'*

B: Experimental Corps of Riflemen, and rifle companies of 60th Regt.
B1: Officer, Experimental Corps of Riflemen, 1800

W.H. Pyne's underestimated but delightful studies, published in 1802, of a battalion baggage waggon being loaded and a column of infantry on the march. There is much to notice, including the headgear—either battered cocked hats or small fatigue caps. Two soldiers wear white trousers, another and a drummer have breeches and short gaiters. Note the tables and other domestic impedimenta thrown in the cart; the sergeant with a halberd; and two soldiers in watch-coats, in the left-hand waggon and walking behind the upper right waggon. (National Army Museum)

B2: Rifleman, Experimental Corps of Riflemen, 1800
B3: Corporal, Rifle Company, 2nd Bn., 60th Regt., 1800

The two-volume work entitled 'English Military Library' of February 1801 provides a plate of the uniform of an 'officer of Colonel Coote Manningham's Experimental Rifle Corps', accompanied by a description as follows: '... *The uniform is a jacket of dark bottle green with a black velvet collar and cuffs, trimmed with black braid and dark green pantaloons and half boots. Their arms and appointments are a helmet, a sabre, a pouch containing a pistol and ammunition. To the pouchbelt is affixed a whistle suspended by a chain, which is used to call the men in performing the different movements and operations of the corps.'* The helmet is shown as the Tarleton pattern with black bearskin crest, a black turban with chains, and a dark green feather; on its right side is a silver stringed buglehorn under a

crown. The plate also shows wings on the jacket, black edged with silver lace and fringe and with a silver curbchain reinforcement. A portrait of Coote Manningham done in 1800 shows a similar costume, but the jacket has no wings and the helmet turban is green. In undress officers wore white duffel jackets edged with green with white waistcoats and white dimity trousers.

The uniforms of the rank and file of either the Experimental Corps or the first uniform of the 95th are shown in drawings prepared as part of Manuals of Rifle Exercise. Each man was issued with '*a green coat without lace, a kersey waistcoat, a cap, a cockade and a tuft and a pair of green pantaloons and half gaiters*'. Corporals had epaulettes or shoulder knots of green and black; sergeants had better-quality clothing, but it is unlikely that they wore any distinguishing badge of rank other than the sash of black, crimson and green stripes. Note that 'tufts' were worn with this uniform, not massive plumes; C.C.P. Lawson noted that many of the drawings prepared for the exercises had been carefully altered, blotting out plumes and reducing the ornament to a small pyramidal tuft.

The rifle companies of the 1st, 2nd, 3rd, 4th and 6th Bns. of the 60th Regiment also wore green. They had single-breasted jackets, the insides of the fronts lined with red and with ten white metal buttons down the front. The short skirts were not turned back but cut sharply away from the fronts, and had diagonal pockets. The collar, cuffs and shoulder straps were also green; the edges were 'feathered' with red, but the coat had no wings or lace. Green pantaloons and half gaiters were the usual nether garments, but the ubiquitous 'mosquito-trousers' illustrated here were worn in the tropical forests of the West Indies.

C: The Light Infantry
C1: Officer, 43rd Regiment, 1812
C2: Sergeant, 52nd Regiment, 1812
C3: Private, 71st Regiment, 1812
In 1800 the 71st Regiment was dressed in Highland costume with kilts and bonnets, although trews were taken into use shortly afterwards. Officers wore pantaloons and half-boots for marches and on campaign. A print by Atkinson illustrates the regiment at Vimiero and shows

The grenadier cap, not normally seen on campaign. The black-laquered plate of white metal was changed to lacquered brass in the first decade of the 19th century. The cap had a red cloth rear patch, and was usually decorated with worsted cap lines and tassels. (National Army Museum)

trews worn over grey socks and buckled shoes, the trews being rather tight and gathered at the ankle by a cord or strap. The brown fur sporran is said to have been worn with the trews for full dress parades and guard mountings. Officers are shown wearing blue pantaloons and Hessian boots. Atkinson shows the feathered bonnet for all ranks. A further print by Clark and Dubourg shows the 71st wearing the kilt and sporran at Vimiero. The tartan for both kilts and trews is the 'Government' or 42nd Regt. sett with white and red overstripes.

When the regiment became Light Infantry there was a correspondence between the Adjutant-General and the colonel of the regiment concerning prospective uniform changes, much of the debate concerning the headdress. The finally approved, sealed pattern was called a 'bonnet cocked'. The pattern has not survived but was probably a cylindrical cap over which the blue knitted bonnet was stretched: however stiffened, the bonnet would not have retained its upright shape without an armature. The bonnet retained its red, green and white dicing around the bottom and was also provided with a black leather peak, tied on with tapes after the fashion of those attached to the feathered bonnets. Some representations show a cockade and a green tuft on the front after the style of the infantry shakos; but Norblin shows a blue bonnet with a diced border, a brass buglehorn, and on the top surface a green 'tourie' or pompon—which seems logical if it was made from a conventional Highland bonnet. In 1810 there is a reference to the diced border and bugle badge being covered with crêpe to deceive the enemy.

There was a contemporary sketch in S.M. Milne's collection by Jones, allegedly executed on campaign, showing an officer wearing a black shako with a cockade and feather and silver buglehorn badge.

The Rev. Gleig, author of 'The Subaltern', who served with the 85th Light Infantry in the Peninsula, described the Light Infantry cap of the period as '... *distinct from the stovepipe infantry cap being slightly lower and smaller at the top and having a brass buglehorn badge. The peak could be worn up or down* ...' In the Oxford Light Infantry Chronicle of 1906 was a photograph of a portrait of Capt. A.M. Douglas wearing such a cap but with a band of material (green, according to Reynolds) around the base of the crown.

More of Pyne's sketches of camp life, dated 1803; the fact that the jackets have lapels in a plate so dated is interesting. Top left, a soldier in a shako with a jug and a clay pipe talks to another wearing the folding fatigue cap. Top right, a soldier in cocked hat and lapelled jacket talks to his woman, who wears a military jacket, while a drummer in a bearskin cap smokes nearby. The other scenes need no explanation, but note the 'band of music' practising at bottom right. (National Army Museum)

London Published May 1. 1803 by Pyne & Nattes.   Drawn & Etch'd by W.H. Pyne.

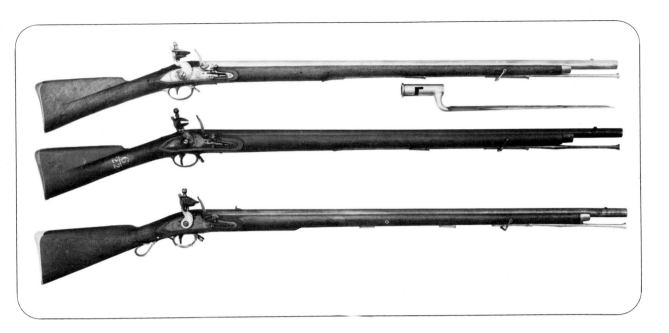

Sergeants of Light Infantry may have developed the custom of wearing chevrons on both sleeves of their jackets—instead of the right sleeve only—shortly after the 1802 order introducing these badges of rank in place of epaulettes and shoulder knots.

Soldiers of the 52nd Light Infantry who had acted with conspicuous bravery during 'Forlorn Hope' attacks were allowed to wear a distinctive badge of '*laurel on the right arms with V.S. (Valiant Stormer) beneath*'. Napier mentions that officers of the 43rd Light Infantry adopted the fashion of wearing grey or scarlet pelisses during the Peninsular campaign, with silk braid. The custom is confirmed by Chichester and Short in their 'Records and Badges of the British Army', and Napier was painted with a pelisse slung from his left shoulder. Note that C2 and C3 wear buff,

The top two muskets are the pre- and post-1809 versions of the India Pattern 'Brown Bess'; the bottom example is the Light Infantry version of the New Land Pattern, with scroll or pistol grip behind the trigger guard, and rudimentary back sight. The barrel is browned. (DOE, Crown copyright)

rather than whitened leather equipment, as members of regiments with buff facings.

D: 95th Rifles
D1: Officer, 95th Regt., 1811
D2: Rifleman, 95th Regt., 1811
D3: Sergeant, 95th Regt., 1811

Officers of the 95th wore full dress coats of dark green with long skirts; the coats were lined with white shalloon, the turned-back skirts with white casimere, sewn down. At the joining of the turn-

The magnificent Baker rifle, the weapon used by the 95th Rifles, the 5/60th during its later service, the élite companies of the KGL Light Bns., and the sharpshooter sections of KGL Line Bns. (DOE, Crown copyright)

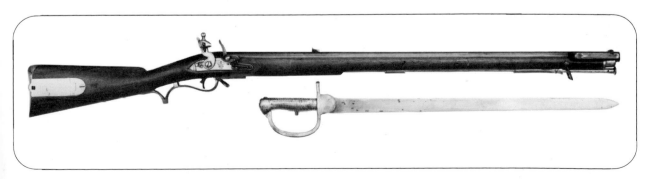

backs was a circlet of black velvet, embroidered silver. The collar, cuffs and lapels were black velvet; the coat had black velvet wings decorated with silver lace, and silver buttons.

The service jacket was similarly dark green and officially described as '*being without lapels or skirts and buttoned over the body to the waist*'. It had a black velvet collar, lined green, and pointed black velvet cuffs with five buttons at the rear seam. There was a double row of buttons down one front, and a single row and button holes down the other. There were 22 buttons in each row, and the same number of black silk twist loops between the rows of buttons, with a knot on each outer side. The loops tapered from $7\frac{1}{2}$ins. at the top of each front, gradually reducing to $2\frac{1}{2}$ins. at the bottom. There was a twist of cord on each collar front, and a row of black braid down the back from shoulders to hip buttons, with a double row on the sides of the fronts instead of pockets. The 1802 regulations specified black velvet wings and shoulder straps, but these seem to have been abandoned by the Peninsula period. The silver buttons were ball-shaped. A dark green pelisse with black silk twist and dark grey (or, apparently, brown) fur trim was also worn.

Field officers and adjutants wore knee-length boots and spurs. In undress officers wore white jackets edged with green, white waistcoats and loose white trousers. The first headdress was a polished black 'cap-helmet' of Tarleton pattern with a dark green pleated turban, silver chains and a green feather. This was subsequently replaced by a cylindrical leather cap with a movable peak or visor worn either up or down; and dark green, black or white cap lines; and a green feather. The figure D1 is based on a water-colour portrait of John Kent which was executed by a brother officer in the Peninsula. Note dagged or 'vandyked' leather reinforce on campaign overalls, and high attachment of their chains.

The sergeant and rifleman are based on a series of watercolours of the regiment; a painting by Denis Dighton; and Atkinson's painting of a rifleman, which was used by P.W. Reynolds in preparing his plate for the Regimental History. Note that some paintings show white pipings and others do not. The sergeant's sash is scarlet with a black stripe. Sergeants and corporals wore white chevrons at this period; the former also carried a cane as a sign of office, looped to a top left-hand button of the jacket. Acting NCOs wore a sword badge on the right arm, and 'chosen men' a band of white cloth around the upper right arm. First class marksmen were distinguished by green cockades, and other riflemen who had completed the marksmanship course by white cockades. From 1807 onwards sergeants wore black collars and cuffs on their grey issue great-coats. In undress the NCOs and men wore white flannel jackets with green collars and cuffs, white waistcoats, loose white trousers, and black forage caps with white edging and lettering, the latter being carried rolled and strapped beneath the cartridge pouch when equipment was worn.

NCOs and men, and in the Peninsula some officers too, carried the Baker rifle. This had a 2ft. 6in. barrel, often browned, and a sword-bayonet which gave it an overall length of 5ft. 10ins.; the rifle weighed 11lbs. 2oz. A distinctive brass-mounted box in the butt opened on the right side; early examples had two interior compart-ments, one for ball ammunition and one for patches. Small tools were also carried in the box, including a 'wiping eye' and a lever which fitted into the screw at the end of the ramrod. A later pattern had the ramrod fitted into a slot in the stock and a smaller, $4\frac{1}{2}$in. butt box. The wooden mallet originally issued for hammering the ram-rod, due to the tight fit of the balls into the rifled barrel, was unpopular and later discontinued.

Personal equipment differed from that of the Line infantry in several respects. The single shoulder belt supported a pouch behind the right hip in the usual manner, this containing made-up paper cartridges for use when a hot action gave no time for loading with separate ball and powder. When conditions allowed, the more accurate method of loading was preferred; a supply of separate ball and patches was carried, both in the butt box and in the small waist belt pouch, and a horn or copper powder flask was carried on a cord strung through leather 'pipes' on the pouch belt.

Under field conditions in the Peninsula there was probably some use of the standard Line infantry grey campaign trousers by Rifle units.

E: The Highland Regiments
E1: Officer, Grenadier Company, 92nd Regt. (Gordon
  Highlanders), 1812
E2: Sergeant, Light Company, 79th Regt. (Cameron
  Highlanders), 1815
E3: Private, Battalion Company, 42nd (Royal High-
  land) Regt., 1815

At Quatre Bras the 92nd was commanded until his death by the popular Lt. Col. J. Cameron, command then passing to Maj. Macdonald; in all five officers were killed and 20 wounded during the battles of Quatre Bras and Waterloo. The 79th was commanded at both battles by Lt. Col. Douglas, despite a knee wound; five officers were killed and 26 wounded in this battalion. The 42nd, Black Watch, lost its Lt. Col., R. Macnamara, at Quatre Bras; he was hacked down after being captured by the French. Maj. R. Dick took command until seriously wounded himself; in all the battalion lost four officers killed and 17 wounded in the 1815 campaign. Rank-and-file casualties for the three battalions in 1815 were respectively 357, 448 and 317.

The 2/73rd fought with Colin Halkett's brigade in Alten's Third Division, and (according to Sgt. Tom Morris) only one officer and some 70 men were left alive and unwounded on the night of Waterloo; Siborne gives casualties as 332 out of 562, however. This unit was not dressed in Highland costume. The 2/78th, a small battalion with a strength of only 337 NCOs and men, formed the Nieuport garrison in 1815.

The headdress of the regiments dressed in Highland costume was the feathered—'mounted'—bonnet (*boineud*). This comprised the blue knitted 'hummel' bonnet, 'cocked up' and covered with black ostrich feathers, probably fixed over a wire cage. Grenadier companies of the 79th and 92nd had white hackles, their Light companies green hackles, and the centre companies white-over-red. In the 42nd the centre companies wore red hackles, and the grenadiers, light infantry, band, and drummers wore white, green, white and yellow feathers respectively, all tipped with red. It is possible that only officers had cut feather hackles, and the rank and file woollen tufts. Detachable black peaks were worn on the bonnet by all Highland regiments at Waterloo, but the two ribbons which hung at the rear of the bonnets

Charles Hamilton Smith's famous plate of 1812 showing a sergeant and a private of the Foot Guards wearing typical winter dress. Note the oilskin covers on the shakos, complete with plume covers; the method of carrying mess tins or camp kettles on the knapsacks; the special pattern water canteens shown for the Guards; and the iron-shod shoes. (National Army Museum)

were not attachment but bonnet tightening tapes. Officers had chin straps as well. A large black cockade was worn at the left side, bearing special badges: e.g. the 42nd had the Sphinx, with additional grenade and buglehorn badges for the flank companies. Diced bands varied, but were usually red, green and white. During the Peninsular War most bonnets were gradually denuded of feathers, and by the end of it many had none. A small woollen tuft was fitted to the front of some blue bonnets in the style of the English shako. Pipers may have had red hackles. A painting by Fischer shows a drummer in 'reversed clothing' wearing a bonnet with a peak, no feathers, and an upright red-over-white feather at the front. Pipes were probably covered in green cloth with ribbons of the facing colour or tartan.

The 42nd, 79th and 92nd all wore the kilt in

Three views of the small folding fatigue cap which appears to have been in universal use among British infantry until late in the Napoleonic Wars; this is the type worn by many soldiers in Sgt. Porter's sketches of the 61st Regiment in Egypt in 1801, and visible—usually spread into a squatter shape by being pulled down on the head—in many of Pyne's and St Clair's drawings. This North Hampshire Militia example, now in the Royal Hampshire Regiment Museum in Winchester, is of white cloth with red tape binding and lettering, now faded to deep pink. (Photos by Martin Windrow, courtesy R. Hants. Regt. Museum)

the Peninsula and at Waterloo. After 1808–09 officers discarded the kilt for active service and adopted pantaloons or trousers of white, grey or blue, worn with Hessian boots or gaiters. For some parades officers of the 42nd wore light blue trousers with broad gold stripes edged scarlet. Officers of the 92nd are said to have worn dark grey pantaloons.

The old belted plaid had been discarded in favour of the 'little kilt', but officers still wore the 'Highland scarf' when on mounted duty or for gala occasions. The rank sashes of both officers and sergeants of Highland regiments were worn over the left shoulder and tied at the right hip.

The 42nd and the 92nd wore Government pattern tartan. The grenadier company, and probably the whole of the 42nd, wore this with a red overstripe until 1812. The 92nd tartan had a yellow overstripe. The 79th wore Cameron of Erracht tartan, devised for them by the mother of Alan Cameron, their first colonel, and based on the Macdonald sett. In the later Peninsular campaigns replacement clothing was so scarce that kilts were not replaced when worn out. There are several records of units being ordered to make their kilts up into trews, for warmth in very cold weather, and once in trews a regiment might retain them for long periods.

Red and white cloth hose were known as 'cadis' or 'cath-dath'. The usual pattern was red and white dicing, edged black for the 42nd and 78th. A form of 'hose top' or footless hose was also worn as an economy measure, and were known as 'moggins'. Short grey or black gaiters were worn over the hose.

Sporrans were not worn on active service. For undress the usual outfit was a short, white, round-bottomed jacket with facing-colour collar and cuffs, and blue bonnets without feathers. The normal service jacket worn by Highland regiments was slightly shorter than that of the English Line infantry, with eight front buttons, and diagonal skirt pockets. Sergeants of the 42nd probably had silver lace, although the 1802 Clothing Review mentions white silk.

F: West India Regiments and 93rd Highlanders
F1: Sergeant, Grenadier Company, 93rd Foot, 1812
F2: Private, 5th West India Regiment, 1812
F3: Officer, 1st West India Regiment, 1812

The 93rd gained a fine reputation during its stay in South Africa. (A number of negroes were employed by the regiment and one returned with it to Britain, probably as a percussionist in the band.) At New Orleans the regiment had a strength of 35 officers and 907 NCOs and men, with 22 drummers; it served in the 3rd Brigade with the 5th West India Regiment, and companies of the 85th Light Infantry, the 43rd Light Infantry and the 95th Rifles. The light company was detached with those of the 7th Royal Fusiliers and 43rd Light Infantry and a detachment of the 1st West India Regiment. The 93rd suffered very badly from disease and battle casualties, and lost nearly three-quarters of its strength. They wore the undress 'hummel' bonnet, with a red and white diced band and a tourie on the top centre, red, white and green for centre, grenadier and light companies respectively. Officers probably wore a silver badge on the front of the bonnet in the form of a spray of thistle with '93' in the centre. Officers' lace was silver with a yellow line, and was in 'bastion' loops. NCOs and men had pointed loops. Officers wore white or grey pantaloons and Hessian boots; the rank and file had their kilts made up into trews before departing on this campaign, but there is evidence that some, at least, wore grey trousers at New Orleans. Company officers and sergeants carried the Highland broadsword frogged from a shoulder belt, and field officers a sabre suspended from slings from a waist belt.

When the so-called 'Black Corps' were first raised from Island Ranger units it was proposed that they should have cavalry troops; six were actually formed, but soon disbanded. Sir John Moore considered the negro regiments to have good qualities, and wrote to Sir Ralph Abercromby to the effect that with proper training they would be 'equal to any problems'. Artillery sections, trained by European NCOs, also existed. The Carolina Corps, which was amalgamated with Malcolm's, later Whyte's, to form the 1st

The effect of firing a smooth-bore muzzle-loading musket on a still day. Note the vivid explosion at the lock, and the thick smoke created by both the priming and the main charge of this original Charleville owned by Geneva collector Nick Michael. Soldiers of the period recorded suffering a raging thirst when they had been in action for long periods. The effect of the saltpetre in the mouth from biting open the cartridges, and the general distribution of burned powder during firing, must have been appalling. The powder deposits a thick film all over the area for several inches all around the lock; hands, faces, and the fronts of clothing and equipment must have been blackened after a few volleys. (Photo by Martin Windrow)

A rich epaulette of the 2nd Foot Guards, c. 1803, showing the laced strap, corded edge, embroidered crown in full colours, padded crescent, spangles and bullion fringe. (**National Army Museum**)

West India Regiment, had both cavalry and infantry elements, and earned a good service record during the American War of Independence. Many negro soldiers of the Carolina Corps formed a Corps of Dragoons, which existed for some time before the 1st W.I. Regt. was properly embodied.

Officers' uniforms of the early period are poorly documented; but Lawson was of the opinion that they wore short double-breasted jackets similar in cut and style to those worn by British infantry in 1812–15. They were probably half-lined. The problem is to decide whether they had the half-lapels worn by the rank and file. Lawson thought this unlikely, although it was prescribed in the 1802 regulations. A portrait silhouette by Buncombe unfortunately fails to answer the question as it is only bust length; and the only other known contemporary painting shows a back view. However, both sources confirm the round hat. Blue or slate-grey pantaloons and Hessian boots

completed the costume, although it seems reasonable to assume that wide-legged white duck trousers would have been worn in undress in the hot season.

The jacket of the rank and file was red (scarlet for NCOs), very short-skirted, and made without turn-backs—it was cut to slope sharply away behind. It had no sleeve lining and only part body lining. It had half-length lapels, but was made to button down to the waist. The stand collar was of ground colour, but the lapels, cuffs and shoulder straps were of facing colour. Three buttons and loops of regimental lace were displayed on each lapel, NCOs wearing white silk lace. The lapels were originally four inches wide at the top, tapering down to three inches at the bottom, but as time passed these became shield-shaped. The description of the jacket in the 1802 regulations has some curious features. The cuffs were two inches deep, 'pointed', and opened with two buttons. Collar, cuffs and shoulder straps were all edged in regimental lace, and there was 'a loop and button on each end of the collar'. There were eight front buttons 'below the lapel'; the skirts are 'well folded over', and there was a button on each hip. Hamilton Smith shows only a few buttons below the lapels, round cuffs with lace loops, and pockets in the sides of the jacket. The explanation is probably that the lapels formed a plastron covering most of a single row of eight buttons 'below'—i.e. behind them.

Loose-fitting white trousers of Russia duck were worn in lieu of waistcoats and breeches. Hamilton Smith's plate shows a small figure wearing these trousers, cut to come well down over the foot, although grey gaiters are worn underneath. In about 1810 blue gaiter-trousers were introduced, and are shown for the 5th Regt. in Hamilton Smith's plate. Regiments were also issued with a short white jacket with collar and cuffs of the facing colour, worn with loose white duck trousers for drill, barrack duties and fatigues. Hamilton Smith shows the 1812 pattern shako with a white 'garland' or cord, brass plate, and white-over-red feather; flank companies would doubtless have worn the usual white and green distinctions.

Oman gives the establishment of the eight regiments as 1,125 all ranks each. The 1st and 5th fought bravely alongside the 93rd Highlanders

Jacket of a Volunteer sergeant, c. 1800, regiment unknown.
Note the unusual pattern of the sleeve chevrons, with the
facing colour appearing in the centre of the lace, instead of
as a backing for it; and the narrowness of the looping on the
breast. The curved cut of the waist would have changed to
a smarter, squarer cut by 1815. (National Army Museum)

	FOOT GUARDS		LINE INFANTRY		FUSILIERS	LIGHT INFANTRY	HIGHLANDERS		RIFLE CORPS
	Centre Company	Flank Companies [1]	Centre Company	Flank Companies [1]			Centre Company	Flank Companies [1]	
Colonel [2]									
Lieutenant Colonel									
Major									
Captain									
Lieutenant or Ensign [1]									
Sergeant Major									
Quarter Master Sergeant									
Drum Major [7]									
Colour Sergeant [4]									
Sergeant [5]									
Lance Sergeant									
Corporal [5]									
Lance Corporal or Chosen Man [5]									

The stylized illustrations opposite represent the shoulder and sleeve insignia of rank worn by officers and men. The symbols used are, e.g.: *Colonel, Foot Guards* = Fringed epaulettes charged with a crown and a star, both shoulders: *Captain, Line Infantry, Flank Companies* = Wings, charged with either a bugle-horn or a grenade, on both shoulders: *Lieutenant or Ensign, Line Infantry, Centre Company* = Fringed epaulette, no devices, right shoulder only: *Major, Fusiliers* = Fringed epaulettes charged with a grenade and a star, above wings, both shoulders; etc, etc.

Notes:

(1) Flank company officers wore either a bugle or a grenade in gold on silver, silver on gold, depending on regimental lace colour.
(2) Adjutants were distinguished by an epaulette on the right and a fringeless strap—contre-epaulette—on the left.
(3) No firm evidence exists to show whether Highland officers wore wings prior to 1815, or whether company officers wore two epaulettes.
(4) Lance sergeants wore white chevrons on jackets of red—i.e., they did not wear scarlet jackets of sergeants' quality.
(5) Regimental lace patterns.
(6) NCOs of the 5th Bn., 60th Regt. wore red chevrons.
(7) In some regiments the drum major wore a crown over his chevrons.
(8) When in full dress only.

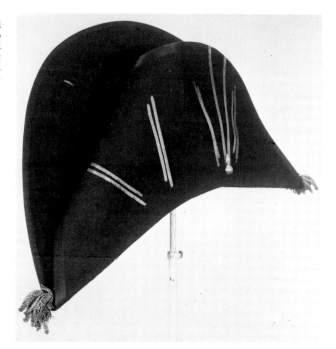

Officer's cocked hat—bicorne—of *c.* 1804, of a black felt material with a black ribbon binding at the edge. The gold 'stay cords' threaded in and out of the hat were used—by pulling the tassels at their ends—to tighten up the front and back panels and keep them upright. The small grenade badge would originally have been on the cockade, no doubt. (National Army Museum)

at New Orleans, suffering heavy losses both from enemy fire and from the weather.

G: *Light Battalions, King's German Legion*
G1: *Sergeant, Scharfschützen/Buchsenschützen, 2nd Light Bn. KGL, 1815*
G2: *Officer, 2nd Light Bn. KGL, 1815*
G3: *Private, 1st Light Bn. KGL, 1815*

Both battalions wore green uniforms faced black, but there were major differences of detail between the two units.

1st Battalion

The headdress of officers, NCOs and men of this unit was a slightly tapered, cylindrical shako with a rectangular peak (movable for officers) and a chin strap. On the front was a silver stringed buglehorn and '1', and a green tuft—woollen for rank and file, cut feather for officers—rising from a black leather cockade. Looped around the cap was a double garland of black or dark green cord with two tassels. For undress, and with the long-tailed coat, field officers wore a cocked bicorne hat with crimson stay-cords, a black silk cockade and a long green feather. Officers wore dark green double-breasted jackets with black velvet collars, pointed cuffs, turn-backs and inside lapels, all trimmed with black silk braid. There were two rows of silver buttons down the fronts,

two at the hips, and five on each diagonal pocket flap; the shoulders were decorated with silver scaled wings on black underlay. NCOs, riflemen and centre company men wore single-breasted jackets with black collars and black round cuffs trimmed with black braid, but green turn-backs—also trimmed with black braid. The jacket had black shoulder straps and large black woolly wings. There were 12 silver buttons down the front, two at the hips, three on each pocket flap, one on the rear seam of each cuff, and one through the oblong flap of a small left breast pocket. All ranks wore grey trousers, the officers' pattern having a single broad silver side-stripe.

2nd Battalion

NCOs and men wore slightly tapered shakos with chin straps, rounded peaks, green ball pompons, and black garlands with tassels. The buglehorn badge had a central '2'. Officers wore the cylindrical *flugelmütze* cap with a movable, detachable peak and with gold and crimson lines. The wing or 'flame' of the cap was worn on campaign and on ordinary parades with the black side showing,

A pioneer of the Foot Guards; on active service the shako would replace the bearskin worn here. Note the pickaxe carried on the back and the bill-hook slung at the hip, the cartridge pouch worn on the waist-belt, and the apron.

braid. There were two (one authority says three) buttons at the hips of the tiny tails. One drawing suggests that there were two breast pockets with flaps and buttons, but these are normally obscured by the breast strap of the knapsack. The jacket had large black woolly tufts or rolls instead of true wings. Trousers were grey, with two silver stripes for officers. The latter could also wear green hussar-type breeches with black braid knots and seams with Hessian boots. On campaign the usual overalls with leather booting were worn, and wide Nankeen trousers were common in hot weather. (The illustration shows green distinctions on the overalls and a gold cockade, both departures from regulation appearing on the actual uniform worn by Hauptmann Georg Wackerhagen when captured at Bayonne in 1814.)

Officers' and sergeants' sashes were crimson; corporals wore green cords and tassels looped from the left shoulder to a breast button. Mounted field officers had dark green saddlecloths edged silver, and bearskin flounces over the holsters. The full dress version had in addition silver crowns and royal cyphers and eight-pointed stars in front and rear corners. The black-lacquered sabretaches had the eight-pointed star device. Overcoats were grey, with green collars and cuffs for sergeants; the sleeved undress waistcoat was white, with green collar, cuffs and chevrons for NCOs. Undress caps were green; those of officers had peaks, those of the NCOs and men light green bands, dark green touries, and no peaks. Hornists —buglers—wore the uniform of the battalions with red collar and cuffs edged with black braid, and green and red woolly wings and bugle-cords. NCOs' rank chevrons were two white, three white, four silver, and four silver below a crown for corporals, sergeants, staff sergeants and sergeant majors respectively.

Note that it was only the élite sharpshooter companies which were armed and equipped as Rifle corps; centre companies were armed with muskets and had black leather musket equipment.

At Waterloo the combined casualties of the two battalions were 347. Their weak starting strength made this a significant loss. Two companies of the 1st, six of the 2nd, and the light company of the 5th Line Bn. were almost wiped out in the stubborn defence of La Haye Sainte farm.

but for levees, galas and other full dress occasions had it reversed to expose white silk lining. The black side displayed a gold edge, the white side a black edge. When the former was exposed a gold, circular, crowned badge was seen on the front of the cap, which normally had a black cockade and green feather.

Officers' jackets resembled those of the 95th Rifles, with black silk braid and silver buttons; there was also some use of pelisses, with black braid and fur. The jackets of the rank and file also resembled those of the 95th, with three rows of silver buttons, 12 in the centre and 15 in the outer rows. The jacket had no turn-backs, being sharply cut away at the waist and edged in black

H: Line Battalions, King's German Legion
H1: Sergeant, Scharfschützen, Light Company, 3rd
  Line Bn. KGL, 1815
H2: Officer, Grenadier Company, 1st Line Bn. KGL,
  1815
H3: Private, Light Company, 2nd Line Bn. KGL, 1815

In 1807 six battalions formed part of Sir William Cathcart's expedition to Copenhagen; the 1st and 2nd formed von Barsse's 3rd Brigade, the 3rd, 4th, 5th and 6th von Drieberg's 2nd Brigade. Gen. Sir John Stuart commanded the 3rd, 4th, 6th and 8th in Sicily in 1808, and the 5th and 7th were at Santarem in 1809. At Waterloo the 5th and 8th Bns. formed part of the 2nd Bde. of the Third Division commanded by Alten, and the 1st, 2nd, 3rd and 4th formed the 1st Bde. of the Second Division commanded by Clinton. The Line battalions lost 23 officers killed during the battle, including Col. du Plat, commanding the 1st Bde., and Ompteda, who commanded the 2nd; 29 officers were wounded. Rank-and-file casualties totalled 738.

The Line battalions were dressed in the same type of uniform as British Line infantry, and their sergeants had similar badges. Before 1812 officers wore the cocked hat and the men the cylindrical shako with the large near-rectangular brass plate and frontal woollen tuft. By 1815 all ranks wore the high-fronted 'Belgic' shako. In the Mediterranean it is likely that they would have worn the ubiquitous 'round' hat; there are references to them wearing 'hats' rather than 'caps'.

Details of the officers' and other ranks' jackets are taken from garments preserved at the Heimatsmuseum, Hanover. Note that although Hamilton Smith shows a Line battalion grenadier with blue wings, like the Foot Guards, a preserved example has red wings. Drummers of the centre and grenadier companies, and the buglers of the sharpshooter section wore red uniforms faced blue with profuse white and blue lace decoration on all seams and in the form of sleeve chevrons. The buglers carried rifles, and had green bugle-cords. Drums were painted blue with the Royal Arms on the front, and had red rims with white 'worms'.

Sharpshooters had white pouch belts with green powder horn cords, white waist belts with snake clasps, sword bayonets, and Baker rifles. Their shakos had green cords and tufts and black chin straps. Sharpshooter sergeants' belts were lacquered, and they carried whistles. Sharpshooter officers had wings with gilded curbchain reinforcement and silver buglehorn badges on the crescents, and buglehorn ornaments on the jacket skirts. They wore pouch belts with lion masks, shields, picker and chain ornaments, and a pouch containing a small pistol; they also carried whistles. Their swords were sharply curved sabres

A bugler of the Foot Guards, showing the manner in which the jacket was embellished with special lace over all seams and down the sleeves in chevrons; the fringed collar was unique to the Guards. Note the size the bugle is depicted.

suspended from narrow waist belts. Their sashes were of Light Infantry pattern—narrow crimson silk items with long tasselled cords brought round the right side and hooked up in front (Buckmaster's pattern book). They wore grey trousers with gold stripes.

The Line battalions had Colours. The first or King's Colour was the Union of the crosses of St George, St Andrew and St Patrick with in the centre, all in gold, 'Kings/ German/ Legion/' over '. . . Battalion', the legend surrounded by a wreath of rose, thistle and shamrock with a large Royal Crown overall. The second or Regimental Colour was of blue silk with the same central motif, and a small Union flag in the upper hoist canton. By 1815 both Colours bore the honour 'Peninsula' in widely spaced gold letters in a curve over the crown.

Notes sur les planches en couleur

A1, A3: D'après des aquarelles faites aux Antilles par Hamilton Smith. Le 5ème Bataillon portait des uniformes verts à revers rouges et le 6ème Bataillon un lisière rouge seulement. Le soldat du 6ème Bataillon a des culottes blanches, portées en régions tropicales. A cette époque les fusils venaient d'Allemagne. **A2:** Notes le casque 'Tarleton' de la caualerie légère.

B1, B2: Très proche de l'illustration précédente, mais notez les revers noirs et le fusil Baker. Les trois rangées de boutons de la veste du soldat allaient demeurer spécifiques au 95ème Régiment de Voltigeurs. **B3:** Comparez avec A3; notez en particulier la frange mélangée (chinée) rouge et verte sur l'épaulette, et la manchette à quatre boutons.

C1: Les caractéristiques de la cavacerue kégère, telle que cette pelisse et le sabre courbe, étaient typiques des officiers de l'Infanterie Légère; notez également les sifflets portés par C1 et C2. **C2:** Les sergents de l'Infanterie Légère avaient des mousquets au lieu des piques de leurs homologues de l'Infanterie de Ligne. Les textes contemporains n'arrivent pas à établir si le shako de l'Infanterie Légère était similaire à celui de l'Infanterie de Ligne ou si c'était un modèle légèrement plus petit et plus pointu. **C3:** Les caractéristiques 'Highland' sont particulières à ce régiment. Le shako était apparemment recouvert d'un béret écossais, d'où la lisière à carreaux et le pompon au sommet.

D1: Notez là encore les traits caractéristiques de la cavalerie légère. La visière carrée du shako pouvait se replier. Remarquez la forme fantaisiste des renforts de cuir de pantalon. **D2, D3:** Le sergent se distingue seulement par les chevrons blancs de la manche droite, son écharpe et sa canne. Une petite corne à poudre pendait d'un cordon vert attaché à le baudrier.

E1: Après environ 1809 les officiers en service actif portaient les pantalons au lieu de 'kilts'. Notez que les officiers et les sergents du Highland portaient l'écharpe indiquant leurs grades sur l'épaule gauche. **E2:** Le béret à plumes a une petite visière attachée par des rubans. Le dessin du 'tartan' de ce régiment était celui du Cameron of Errracht. **E3:** Les plumes de ce béret étaient probablement mises en place à l'aide d'une cage de fils de fer. Le petit insigne sur la cocarde variait de régiment en régiment; ici le Sphynx évoque la campagne d'Egypte en 1801. Le 42ème, 'Black Watch', portait des 'kilts' appelés 'Government Sett' (un 'sett' étant le dessin d'un 'tartan').

F1: S'il faisait froid, les régiments se coupaient souvent des pantalons, 'trews' (braies) dans leurs kilts. Les sergents de toutes les unités avaient des piques. Ici, le béret est 'à nu', sans plumes. **F2:** Le trait particulier de cet uniforme des unités antillaises était le revers à milongueur. **F3:** Le chapeau rond était couramment porté par les officiers servant dans les tropiques.

G1: Les voltigeurs de la Légion Allemande du Roi portaient des uniformes similaires à ceux de 95ème mais plus décorés. **G2:** Notez le shako à la visiere repliée, si semblable au 'mirleton' des hussards. **G3:** Notez la poche gauche de poitrine, très inhabituelle à l'époque; aussi, les petites différences dans les revers. Seule la compagnie de tireurs d'érences dans les revers. Seule la compagnie de tireurs d'élite de chaque régiment avait des fusils. Tandis que les autres avaient des mousquets, comme c'est le cas ici.

H1, H2, H3: Chez le Légion Allemande du Roi des bataillons de Ligne de 1815 portaient des uniformes très similaires à ceux de tout autre régiment 'Royal' anglais, avec des revers bleus. Il y avait de petites différences d'insignes, et la section des tireurs d'élite était une particularité de ces bataillons.

Farbtafeln

A1, A3: Von Aquarellen aus dem Leben, gemalt in den westindischen Inseln von Hamilton Smith. Das 5th Bn. trug grüne Uniformen mit rot besetzt, die 6. trägt nur rote Paspelierung. Der Soldat der 6th trägt die weissen in den Tropen getragenen Hosen. Die Gewehre waren zu diesem Zeitpunkt von deutscher Herstellung. **A2:** Der 'Tarleton' Helm war der der leichten Kavallerie zu diesem Zeitpunkt.

B1, B2: Sehr ähnlich dem vorhergehenden Gemälde, aber bemerke die schwarzen Besätze, und Baker Gewehr. Die dreier-Knopfreihen an der Soldatenjacke bleiben eine Eigenart des Rifle Regiments der 95th Foot. **B3:** Vergleiche mit A3; bemerke die eigenartig gemischten rot/grünen Fransen an den Schulterstücken, und vierknöpfiger Armelaufschlag.

C1: Leichte Kavallerie Besonderheiten, wie diese pelisse und der gebogene Säbel, waren typisch für Light Infantry Offiziere; bemerke auch die Pfeifen, die von C1 und C2 getragen werden. **C2:** Light Infantry Feldwebel trugen Musketen anstelle der Piken ihrer Gegenüber in der Linieninfanterie. Es gibt Meinungsverschiedenheiten in zeitgenössischen Aufzeichnungen darüber, ob das 'Leichte Infanterie Shako' dasselbe war als das zur selben Zeit von der Linieninfanterie getragene oder eine etwas kleinere mehr spitz zulaufende Art. **C3:** Die speziellen Highland Besonderheiten waren eine Eigenart dieses Regiments. Eine Schottenmütze soll über das Shako gestülpt worden sein, deshalb das karierte Band und der Büschel oben in der Mitte.

D1: Wiederum, bemerke die typischen leichten Kavallerie-Merkmale. Der quadratisch geschnittene Schirm des Shako konnte zusammengefaltet werden. Bemerke die phantasievoll geschnittene Lederverstärkung an den Uberziehosen. **D2, D3:** Der Feldwebel unterscheidet sich nur durch seine weissen Winkel am rechten Armel, seine Schärpe und seinen Stock. Ein kleines Pulverhorn hing von einer grünen Kordel, die am Munitionsbeutel befestigt war.

E1: Nach dem Jahr 1809 trugen die Offiziere Uberziehhosen anstelle des kilt wenn im Felddienst. Bemerke, die Rangschärpe über der linken Schulter von Highland Offizieren und Feldwebeln getragen. **E2:** Die gefiederte Haube hat einen kleinen mit Bändern festgebundenen Schirm. Der tartan in diesem Regiment war das Muster 'Cameron of Erracht'. **E3:** Die Federn an der Haube waren wahrscheinlich über einem Drahtgestell angebracht. Das kleine Abzeichen an der Kokarde unterschied sich von Regiment zu Regiment—hier, die Sphinx, bedeutet Dienst in Egypten im Jahr 1801. Die 42nd—'Black Watch'—trug Kilts nach dem Muster, bekannt als 'Government sett' (ein sett ist ein Schottenmuster).

F1: In kaltem Wetter war es in den Regimentern üblich, aus ihren kilts Hosen —'trews'—herzustellen. Linieninfanterie-Feldwebel aller Einheiten trugen Piken. Hier ist die Haube 'unmounted'—ohne Federn. **F2:** Das Hauptmerkmal der Uniform der westindischen Einheiten war der Aufschlag, zur halben Länge geschnitten. **F3:** Der runde Hut war sehr üblich für Offiziere in tropischen Feldzügen.

G1: Die Scharfschützen der King's German Legion trugen Uniformen ähnlich der der 95th Foot, jedoch mehr ausgeschmückt. **G2:** Bemerke das Shako mit zusammengefaltetem Schirm, einem Hussaren mirleton sehr ähnlich. **G3:** Bemerke die linke Brusttasche—sehr ungewöhnlich zu diesem Zeitpunkt; ebenso die kleinen Unterschiedlichkeiten der Besätze. Nur die Scharfschützenkompanie eines jeden Bataillons war mit Gewehren bewaffnet, der Rest—wie hier—mit Musketen.

H1, H2, H3: In den meisten Fällen trugen die Linien-Bataillone der KGL von 1815 dieselben Uniformen wie die von jedem englischen 'Royal' Regiment getragenen mit blauen Besätzen. Es gab nur kleine Unterschiedlichkeiten der Abzeichen; und der Zug der Scharfschützen war eine Eigenart dieses Bataillons.